CLASSIC IRISH HOUSES OF THE MIDDLE SIZE

CLASSIC
IRISH HOUSES
OF THE
MIDDLE SIZE

Maurice Craig

ashfield
PRESS

First published in 1976
Reprinted 1977
©Maurice Craig 1976

Published in 2006 by
ASHFIELD PRESS
DUBLIN • IRELAND

ISBN: 1 901658 56 2

Designed by Susan Waine, Ashfield Press

First published in the U.S.A. in 1977 by Architectural Book
Publishing Co., New York

Library of Congress Cataloging in Publication Data

Craig, Maurice James.
Classic Irish houses of the middle size.

Bibliography: p. Includes index.
1. Architecture, Domestic—Ireland. 2. Neoclassicism (Architecture)—Ireland.
3. Architecture, Domestic—Designs and plans. I. Title.
NA7337. C73 1977 728.8'3'09415 76-49536
ISBN 0-8038-0044-4

TYPESET BY Ashfield Press in 12.5 on 15pt Bembo
PRINTED IN IRELAND BY ßetaprint Limited

FRONTISPIECE Ballysallagh, Johnswell, Co. Kilkenny

CONTENTS

To the Happy Few

Of the photographic illustrations, acknowledgement is due to the *Buildings of Ireland Record* for 9, page 80, 6, 7, page 168; to the Ulster Museum for 11, page 196; to the *National Trust* (Northern Ireland Committee) for 88, page 160; to The Irish Architectural Archive, *Hugh Doran Collection* for 77, page 154, 83, 84, page 158, 85, 86, page 159, 87, page 160, 1, page 164, 13, page 172, 22-28, pages 176-79; The Irish Architectural Archive, *William Garnerman* and *An Foras Forbartha Collections* for 1, page 14, 1, page 64, 54, page 108, 59, page 112, 15, page 123, 24, 25, page 128, 51, page 142, 75, page 153, 15, page 173, 4, page 191; to the *Knight of Glin* for 3, page 39, 16, page 84, 38, page 98; to The Irish Architectural Archive, *Patrick Rossmore Collection* for 6, 8, page 79, 26, page 89, 42, page 102, 46, page 104, 55, page 109, 16, page 123, 17, page 124, 21, page 126, 32, page 132, 60, page 145, 29, page 179; to the *Royal Irish Academy* for 14–16 pages 54–59; to the *Commissioners of Public Works* for 5, 6, page 66; to *N. W. English* for 1, page 68; to *Roger Hill* for 5, page 78; and to *Peter Simpson* for 5, page 161. The remaining photographs are by the author.

The authorship of drawings is stated in the captions. Those by *William Garnerman* are reproduced by permission of *An Foras Forbartha* (Conservation and Amenity Advisory Service), Dublin. All drawings not otherwise acknowledged are by the author. The material on which 47-49, page 105 are based was supplied by the Office of Public Works (Parks and Monuments Division).

REPORT

URING THE THIRTY YEARS since this book was written, there have been, regrettably but predictably, some losses. Sixteen houses have, for one reason or another, disappeared, either engulfed in expanding suburbs,or losing their role and their attraction because they have lost their land. Among them must be numbered Platten (page 38), Kilmacurragh (page 78), Allenton (page 83), Mantua (page 120), Killininny (page 137), Bellevue (page 169), Bloomfield (page 195), Annaghlee (page 144), Crannagh (page 151), Wilton (page 167), Ballynure (page 170), Bowen's Court (page 174), Delaford (page 193), Beech Park (page 194) and Windy Arbour (page 175).

In some of these cases the houses were deliberately allowed to fall into neglect, or were sold and/or demolished by the purchaser. In one case there was a fire, and in one prominent instance the owner simply and under-standably lost heart. For several of them the outlook was already poor thirty years ago. Either they stood on land which could be profitably reused, or they were manifestly unsuitable to the present owner's needs, or they were simply regarded as a nuisance and best out of the way.

Those which were already in ruin are a different matter. They held even less attraction for their owners. They include Brazeel (page 65), which was supposedly under government protection when its owner destroyed it, (reportedly) Lowberry (page 68), Cuba Court (page 94), a loss particularly to be lamented, and Dollardstown (page 106).

Some houses have been injudiciously altered, or have been added to, or have been over-restored, in ways which do not seem to me to have added to their appeal. They include Corbally (page 80), Shannongrove (page 74) and Mount Gordon (page 136), while at Beechlawn (page 197), a new house has been planted directly in front of the old one.

But there has been, during these thirty years, a perceptible change in the economic and cultural context. Some houses previously disregarded have become interesting, not only to incomers with money, but also to local residents who, against all the apparent odds, have given them new life. Such are, among others, Ledwithstown (page 98) and Gaulstown (page 101). We must hope that this very encouraging trend will continue.

There remain some ruined or fragmentary examples about which up-to-date information is lacking. They may still be there, or they may have been tidied away. They include Graney (page 64), Goresgrove (page 71), Kiltullagh (page 88), Piedmont (page 105), Garrettstown (page 104), Tober (page 107) and Lissenhall (page 139). Many more are still to be investigated, especially in the midland counties.

I MARCH 2006

PREFACE

I T IS RELATED OF AN EMINENT French automobile historian that
he was asked by an interviewer: 'It is true, is it not, that you are really
interested only in cars with overhead camshafts?'

'True.'

'And, of those, the cars which truly command your devotion are those
with two overhead camshafts?'

'That also is true.'

The attentive reader of this book will soon be aware that there is a
certain bias behind the selection of examples. It could hardly be otherwise.
There may be more than one opinion about what constitutes the central
tradition in Irish housebuilding. I trust that the core of that tradition has
not gone unrepresented, though the interpretation of it must perforce be
personal.

The body of writing which invites a readership of non-architects to
look at buildings with a critical interest is of fairly recent growth, and is not
yet large. This is especially true of Ireland where the total stock of buildings, though much richer than most people suppose, is still rather limited,
and the critical public more limited still. In such circumstances the writer
may feel a duty to cast his net as wide as possible and to try to bring everything in. This temptation I have tried to resist.

With one exception, no house treated of in Messrs Guinness and
Ryan's *Irish Houses and Castles*[1] is dealt with in this book. Nor does it deal
with that equally important stratum of vernacular building explored by
Estyn Evans and Kevin Danaher.[2] The middle ground between these fields
is large indeed: in chronological terms I have treated it as beginning in
about 1620 and ending in about 1800 or a little later. I have ruled out town
houses and suburban houses, though one or two are included which are
now in suburban situations. I have, so far as possible, tried to avoid houses
of complex origin, and have concentrated on those which seem to be the
product of a single designer working out a single architectural conception

at a particular time. I have disregarded the present condition and prospects of each house: some have disappeared, some are in ruin, some are derelict, some are unsuitably occupied, some adequately, some are maintained with loving care, some few have suffered from an excess of zeal over discretion.

If I have laid what some readers may think to be undue emphasis on certain buildings which may appear small, insignificant and not very exciting to look at, it is because I believe that they are essential links in the chain of evolution. And if, at the other end of the spectrum, I have little to say about the decorative and associational aspects of some rather grander houses, it is because my purpose is to show their relationship to humbler and earlier buildings.

Some of my readers will be unaccustomed to finding so much attention given to plan-forms and structure, and so little to decoration and especially interior decoration.

Most published writing about Irish buildings has, so far, tended to cluster about certain polarities: at one end about the polarities of archaeology and anthropology, and at the other about those of connoisseurship and the history of the fine arts. But since there now exist these two healthy and growing traditions, it seems to me more than time that an effort should be made to bring them together, as it were, under one roof.

Though some of the material was gathered thirty years ago, it would have been impossible to write this book without the generous co-operation of friends, notably William Garnerman, David Griffin, Edward McParland, John O'Connell and the Knight of Glin.

Others whose help it is a pleasure to acknowledge include the following: Charles Acton, Alexandra Artley, Mark Bence-Jones, Adrian Brookholding-Jones, Kevin and Christa Byrne, Mr Cassidy of the Pembroke Estates Management Ltd, Michael Craig, Anne Crookshank, Kevin Danaher, Richard Dann, Hugh Dixon, N. W. English, Peter Ferguson, George Gossip, John Griffith, the Hon Mariga Guinness, Peter Harbison, John Harris, Roger Hill, David Newman Johnson, Keith Kneebone, Howard Konikoff, Denis Lamoureux, Mark Leslie, Rolf Loeber, Gillies McBain, Robert McIntosh, Robert McKinstry, Brian Molloy, Derry O'Connell, G. Wilson Reside, Patrick Rossmore, Alistair Rowan, Peter Simpson, Henry Wheeler and Jeremy Williams, and all owners of houses.

1976

PART I

INTRODUCTION

THE HOUSES TO WHICH I have given most attention are inevitably a very small selection. They have been chosen for a combination of their architectural quality and their significance in the typology of the subject. Some are here as examples of a characteristic type. They have not been chosen for the quality of their decoration; some of them, indeed, can hardly be said to have any decoration at all. I think that the purely architectural qualities which appeal most to me will proclaim themselves clearly enough through the illustrations and more especially through the drawings.

An unhappily high proportion of the houses illustrated in this book have either disappeared or have been mutilated or have fallen into disrepair. There are three reasons for this. One is that there seems to be a baleful correlation between architectural quality and misfortune. Too often it is the best buildings which fall victim to malice, neglect, ignorance, poverty or some amalgam of these evils; or to what can be worst of all, uncertainty of title especially when combined with bucolic paranoia. A second reason is that when a house is threatened or destroyed, the least we can do for it is to record its qualities, since it can no longer speak for itself. Finally, there are times when the dereliction of a house gives opportunities for investigating, measuring and anatomising it, which would not occur if it were in normal occupation.

It is clear that the scope of this book must exclude the 'great houses', such as those, mostly well known, which have been accorded some fitting attention in fittingly sumptuous books. But the 'big house' of Irish traditional ways is not always very large: the term denotes the fact that it was the house of a substantial, and usually resident, landowner, rather than its mere size. As well as these 'big houses', there were and are considerable numbers of houses, built by or lived in by minor gentry or prosperous farmers, or by manufacturers and traders, or occupied as dower-houses, agent's houses or as glebe-houses. The gulf between the 'big house' and the cottage has perhaps been over-emphasised by historians, and too much has been made of the absence of a middle class.

The gulf, on the other hand, between the tower-house-castle of the late Middle Ages, which was the ordinary residence of the minor gentry in the 15th and 16th centuries, and continued to be built down to the middle of the 17th, and the unfortified 18th- and 19th-century house, is real enough. But even then, it is not as complete as it is sometimes thought to be. The accident that almost every surviving 17th-century Irish house is, for one reason or another, a ruin, tends to obscure the quantity of evidence they provide about the transition from 'castle' to 'house'. As for the transition in size and pretension from the cottage to the big house, it would be easy to provide a series of, say, thirty examples, in which, by almost imperceptible stages, one would be led from the humblest of single-storey thatched cabins to the splendours of Russborough. Even farmhouses sometimes have wings, and some great houses have attached farm-buildings, as they have in Denmark.

THE 17TH CENTURY

EVEN THE SMALLEST OF THE HOUSES here treated are large by comparison with the absurd containers we inhabit today. But they were nonetheless small by the standards of their time. As a general rule, the further back in time (at least in the period under review), the more massive the construction. Sometimes this is the only available criterion of date. In the case of Graney (see 1-2, page 64), Co. Kildare, for example, or Derrin, Co. Laois, the argument runs as follows: this building cannot be of the 18th, still less of the 19th century, therefore it must be of the 17th. And why not of the 16th? For no better reason than economy of hypothesis: it is probable in the 17th; in the 16th it is still possible but much less probable to suppose an apparently undefended house of this size.

There remains the possibility that we believe 17th-century buildings to have been of stouter construction because only those of stouter construction have survived. No doubt there is truth in this. No doubt there was once a very much larger number of 17th-century houses than now survive (such as those wide-eaved buildings ubiquitous in Francis Place's drawings)[3] and many of these must have been 'small' by the standards we are using here, and of these some may have been flimsily constructed. But the general tenor of the evidence, both in Ireland and in Britain, suggests that, on the whole, early work is robust.

It is obvious that surviving domestic buildings become increasingly numerous after 1700, and especially after about 1715, and it is also obvious that they have much in common with their counterparts in Britain. Their ancestry derives in part from an influx of settlers, and in part from the local practice of the previous century. Thus both Shannongrove (1–4, pages 74–77) and Yeomanstown (54, page 108), of similar date though widely separated, have in common with Tober, Co. Wicklow (see 52, page 107), Piedmont, Co. Louth (48, page 105) (both roughly contemporary) and with Graney (much earlier) the spacing of their windows very far from the corners. Shannongrove and Yeomanstown have also in common the use of brick (always rare in Ireland except in Dublin and later in Belfast), the steep roofs to be expected at the time, and the use of 'Dutch' gables in a subsidiary role. The patterning of the chimney-stacks at Shannongrove harks back, almost uniquely in Ireland, to the England of Wolsey's Hampton Court. But the setting of lofty shafts diagonally in a stack, found so late as Greenfield at Milltown, Co. Dublin, which from its plan can hardly be much before 1700, goes back in Irish usage at least to Derryhivenny (1643)[4] and no doubt to the 16th century, when it was, of course, commonplace in England.

THE TRANSITION

SOME OF THE LARGER 16th- and 17th-century houses are of the expanded tower-house with-flankers type. Such are Rathfarnham, Kanturk, Raphoe and Portumna.[5] At Portumna the staircases were, most exceptionally, in the main body: at Kanturk the single staircase was in one of the flankers. Other large houses – large by Irish standards – such as Coppinger's Court and Mallow,[6] had complicated projections with a strong tendency for the staircase or staircases to be in one or more of the projections. The cruciform houses, such as Ightermurragh and Kilmaclenine,[7] are not really cruciform: they are rectangles with a porch sticking out in front and a staircase-tower sticking out behind. Farther down the scale of size come the L-plan and T-plan houses, such as Fennor, Killincarrig, Castle Baldwin, Graney, Ballincar, Ballyloughan, Ballyduff and many others; and here, too, the projection contained the stairs.

The idea of the stairs being contained within the rectangular outline seems to have taken a long time to sink in.[8] In part, this preference for complex outlines was of defensive origin: it is wasteful of materials and of heat, but it is marginally easier to defend with crossfire. In part it seems to have been a process analogous to that by which the bonnet or engine-house, and the spare tyre, were only gradually absorbed into the enveloping shell of the motor-car, or the simplification of syntax in such a language as English. As late as the mid-1770s such a house as Cuffesborough[9] shows a plan which is still 17th-century in essence. By the same token, gables took longer to fade away from the backs of houses than from the fronts.

The compact double-pile house arrived in Ireland very little later than in England. The early examples[10] must have been near Dublin and have vanished, except for Beaulieu, Co. Louth. Eyrecourt in County Galway, which has now almost disappeared,[11] is smaller than Beaulieu and conforms completely to the Hugh May type of compact house, as did Molyneux House, a still smaller free-standing house in the city of Dublin which survived until the early 1940s. Molyneux House, from before 1710, was almost exactly contemporary with the Tailors' Hall, which has a staircase-tower projecting at the rere and other archaic features.

Much though two houses may resemble one another in plan, they may differ greatly in their expression by reason of one being gable-ended while the other is hip-roofed. This dichotomy has long been noticed in the humblest type of dwelling (see the 'central-hearth' and 'gable-hearth' types illustrated by E. E. Evans,[12] who makes a correlation between the end-hearth and gable-end on one hand, and the central-hearth and hip-roof on the other, and states that gable-ended houses are universal in the North, found side-by-side with the half-hip in the Midlands, and side-by-side with fully hipped examples in the South).

The territory which this book seeks to explore is that extending from the cottage or cabin to the minor country house. This territory contains some houses which have gable-ends, and rather more which have roofs hipped all round. There is, with these houses as with the cottages, a tendency for end-gables to go with the possession of fireplaces and stacks in the end walls. There is also a tendency for the gable-end to become rarer towards the upper end of the social scale. The expression a 'farmhouse' conjures up such a building as Clonbrogan (75, page 153) or Killininny (41, page 137), both gable-ended. Conversely, it is almost impossible to imagine a house of the grandeur of, say, either of the Castletowns showing a gable on any of its faces.

Yet, marked as the tendency may be, it is still only a tendency. The gable-end is, or was, found much higher in the social scale than is commonly realised. Belan House, Co. Kildare, the large seat of a noble family, had gable-ends, and the examples of Yeomanstown (54, page 108), Sherwood Park (47, page 140) and others may be adduced. High Park, Kiltegan, Co. Wicklow, has an unusual combination of a hipped roof with gable-ends.

Mount Hanover and Dysart, two houses with very similar plans, are instructive in this respect. To judge by the details, Mount Hanover (61–62, page 114) must be of the first third of the 18th century, or perhaps as late as about 1740, while Dysart (35-37, pages 134-35) is of 1757. At Mount Hanover the front half of the house is served by end-stacks on the gables, and the two apse-ended rooms in the back half are served by stacks with their own subsidiary gables in the rere façade, much like those at Newhall, Co. Clare. At Dysart, by contrast, all the flues are gathered together into two central stacks standing on arches (as at Castletown Conolly), in spite of the fact that those of the back rooms are in the virtually windowless back wall. To achieve this result, the flues had to be led horizontally through thick walls. Towards the end of the 18th century it is not uncommon to find quite size-able houses with one very massive single central stack serving every hearth in the house. Perhaps the most extreme example known to me is Ballinafad, Co. Mayo; but there are many other instances only a little less striking.

At all periods the stack or stacks were regarded as important elevational elements: most markedly, of course, in the houses with hip-roofs and eaves, but also in the rarer parapeted houses where the roof-slope is a less promi-nent feature. Though care was naturally taken to balance the stacks as elements in the silhouette, it is worth noting that even an accomplished architect happily allowed an extra stack to appear in an eccentric position: good examples are Lismore, Co. Cavan (23, page 88) and Cuba Court, Co. Offaly (32–37, pages 94-97), both of which may well have been designed by Sir Edward Lovett Pearce (*circa* 1699-1733).

It would be too much to claim that the end-gable house and the hip-roofed house with central stack or stacks are merely the corresponding cottage-types writ large. They are obviously something more, and in a sense perhaps also something less. It has been the custom to regard the 'great house' and the 'cabin' as having had little or nothing to do with one another; to pretend that they represented two mutually uncomprehending cultures, occupying the same time and space. This simplistic view has already been undermined on the purely historical front. The sheer numbers of medium-sized and small houses surviving from the 18th century refute this thesis by their very existence, and stylistic continuity between small buildings and large speaks for itself.

It is clear from the researches of D.M. Waterman that even in the counties most thoroughly penetrated by the early 17th-century plantation, the planters, who were in a settlers-and-Injuns situation, and would no doubt ideally have wished to build themselves pure Scotch or English houses (with due provision, to be sure, for defence), were sometimes obliged to use Irish masons, and that it was not long before building 'went native'. Ireland is a flat country, with a much greater measure of geological homogeneity than, for example, England, and it does not take long for an aspect of building technique to penetrate at least the lowland areas of the whole island.

This is well illustrated by a comparison of Brazeel, a house in north County Dublin, as described by H. G. Leask, with two examples some seventy-five miles to the west, in Connacht beyond the Shannon, but in the same century. Leask[13] describes Brazeel, which was built in the 1630s for a Lord Chancellor of Ireland, thus:

> The wall masonry is covered externally with thin plaster, lightly rough-cast and of the finest quality. On the quoins and around the openings the plaster is brought to a finer surface and to a block-and-start design.

This exact finish is still to be seen at Brazeel and also at Portumna Castle, built just before 1618, and at Eyrecourt, built some time in the 1660s, both in County Galway. Leask comments on the resistance of this finish to the Irish climate, as well he might, since all three buildings (and Oldbawn, Co. Dublin which had it also) have been derelict for long periods.

It is unnecessary to labour those aspects of stylistic transition in which Ireland closely follows England, such as, for example, the yielding of stone mullions to mullions of timber, and of these in turn to the double-hung sash. In Ireland, as in parts of England, the mullion-and-transom window lingered on in basements and out-offices long after its banishment from the front proper.

PLAN-TYPES AND THEIR EVOLUTION

WE DO NOT YET KNOW ENOUGH about the internal planning of 17th-century houses to generalise with much confidence. Some useful pioneer work has been done by Mr D. M. Waterman,[13] but most of the buildings which he examined, and most of those I have been able to examine, are ruined; so that though stone dividing-walls may have survived, partitions of timber have not, and their positions can often only be conjectured. Occasionally the 'ghost' of a partition survives as a clue, e.g. at Castle Baldwin (7, page 66).

The simple rectangular plan appears, as we have seen, rarely in the 17th century, as at Brazeel. On an even smaller scale, a house at Toberadora, Co. Tipperary, consisting only of two rooms on each floor, may perhaps be another candidate. It measures only 28 feet 6 inches by 22 feet 9 inches, externally. Though built of stone, it has no dateable features, but the facts that the part of the single stack (in one end gable) which projected above the roof is of red brick, and that the ground-floor fireplace still has a timber bressumer carried on red brick piers, suggest a date near 1700: a time at which, it will be remembered, the peasantry lived in impermanent huts of which no specimen now probably survives. Rudimentary though it be, this little house at Toberadora, having its dividing wall built of stone, looks forward to the 18th century rather than back to the 17th. It is difficult to suppose it much later or much earlier than 1700. It lacks the massive well-crafted masonry which can mislead one into supposing a 19th-century ruin in, for example, County Carlow to be of the 17th.

The plan, which is essentially one-room thick, is a persistent one, and is found surprisingly high up the social scale, as for example Cuffesborough, Vianstown (7, page 120), or Sherwood Park (46-47, page 140). During the

17th century there is a limited number of long narrow houses such as Carstown, Co. Louth, Mosstown, Co. Longford and Clonfert Palace; but not a great deal is known about their anatomy.[14] It is, perhaps, instructive to compare and contrast two houses built probably within twenty years of one another: Brazeel *circa* 1635[15] and Newtownstewart *circa* 1615.[16] They are comparable in size: Brazeel 49 feet by 39 feet, Newtownstewart 45 feet square, in both cases exclusive of projections. Both are divided into two by solid walls, and both, rather illogically, have three gables corresponding to the dimension bisected by the medial wall. In both cases the surviving decorated chimney-stack is built of brick. But whereas at Brazeel the only projections are chimney-breasts containing, at one end, an oven, and the stairs were contained in the rectangle, at Newtownstewart there were two external staircases, one of which is contained in a circular tower less than half engaged in the wall: an obvious importation from Scotland. There is also, at the north corner of the building, a lower wing-like extension which, if it could be shown to have had a counterpart at the east corner (which no longer exists) would look very much like an 'overlapping wing' as found at Jigginstown, Waringstown and Buncrana.

Brazeel was built near Dublin for a Lord Chancellor of Ireland and has, naturally enough, no defensive features whatever. Newtownstewart was built by a settler, Robert Newcomen, in the disturbed province of the North, probably twenty years earlier, yet one pistol loop is the only defensive feature now to be seen there.

Fixing our attention on the primitive rather than the provably early in date, we may turn to Piedmont, Cooley Penninsula, Co. Louth (47-49, page 105). It appears at first sight to be a one-room-thick plan, and so it is, except that there was apparently a lean-to at the back, or to be more precise, two lean-tos, since the staircase-windows must have opened on to a narrow court between the two arms of the U. It is a perplexing house, full of anomalies. On the one hand, it has a mature doorcase and a mature cornice, neatly returned at the ends of the façade, and, of course, symmetry. On the other hand, the proportions of the upper windows for which the cornice serves as lintel, are ungainly; and though at first sight the plan with central hall and flanking rooms seems very advanced, it looks much less so when we realise that the 'hall' is a room with a corner fireplace, and the staircase is in one corner of the room to the right. Such planning is so primitive that we have great difficulty in imagining the kind of owner for whom such a house would have been built: so discriminating in some respects, so easily satisfied in others. In the 18th century it belonged to the Fortescue family, but they had two other houses in County Louth, and this can surely never have been their principal seat.

With Carrownacon near Moore Hall in County Mayo (12-13, page 122) we have a mid-18th-century formal statement of the tripartite single-pile plan, with all the organs in their expected places. Another house, Kiltullagh, Co. Galway, is a double-pile and, though quite classical in demeanour, is impressively furnished with pistol-loops (24-25, pages 88). Though now a ruin it still has its outer walls and its great stacks, and it is possible to determine the pitch of the roof and to appreciate what a handsome house it must have been.

Once the deep rectangle, approaching a square, has been established, there are two obvious ways of dividing it:

the spine-wall system

and the tripartite system

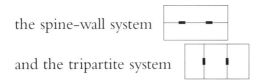

Clearly it is also possible to use both at once thus: , but this is usually unnecessary, since the area of walling required to support two stacks is not very great. The tripartite plan predominates, and though both it and the spine-wall plan are found in the 18th century, the tripartite tends to gain ground as the century advances. No doubt this is why it is commoner, because there are more surviving houses from the later period.

The more space is taken from the entrance-hall and given to the flanking rooms, the closer together will the stacks be, until in extreme cases they are too close together to dominate the elevation, and sometimes create an effect almost of meanness. Early 19th-century farmhouses and glebe-houses sometimes betray the fact that the passage-hall has been straitened in the interests of economy.

Of course if the stacks are put in the outer walls, the entire picture changes, and this is what has happened in a limited number of cases: Bogay, for example, or Woodlands (28–30, pages 90–92), where the determining factor is the structure which rises through the centre of the house to carry the external brick lantern or gazebo. Everything else is subordinated to this. At first sight Ledwithstown (38–40, pages 98–100) might appear to be a spine-wall or double-pile plan, but in fact the transverse walls are not prolongations of each other, and the plan is best understood as a scaled-down version of the 'reflecting staircase' plan as found at, for example, Cashel Palace, and other houses of the Pearce-Castle school. The same applies, on a somewhat larger scale, at Clonbrock, Co. Galway. In fact, at both Ledwithstown and Clonbrock, there are fireplaces in a transverse wall, in a longitudinal wall, and in an outer wall.

Roundwood (17-21, pages 124-26) which is about the same date as Ledwithstown or a little later, cannot be easily classified as either spine-wall or tripartite. Like Dysart, it has fireplaces in the back wall as well as elsewhere.

Later, in the early 19th century, a type of tripartite plan appeared in which, owing to the great depth of the house, a large, wasteful but extremely pleasant hall takes up one-third of the ground floor and also one-third of the upper floor, with the staircase at the back of it. Bermingham, Tuam, Co. Galway (51-52, pages 142-43) approximates to this type. As far as I recall, Bowen's Court of 1776 had such a plan, and Halston (13–14, page 198-99) is a later example. The architecturally treated central upstairs lobby off which the bedrooms are situated, so characteristic a feature of the larger Irish houses, is almost absent from the smaller ones.

A great many houses have a T-plan, which is sometimes the result of a new house having been built on to the end of an old one and at right-angles to it, as, for example, at Beechwood, Co. Tipperary, at Allenton and at Lisrenny, Co. Louth (where the later, larger house has recently been removed), and sometimes the result of an original intention to build to a T-plan, analogously to the 17th-century practice but on a larger scale, as at Youngstown, Co. Kildare, where the staircase is at the junction of the stem with the bar of the T, or at Castle Blunden, Co. Kilkenny (16, page 123).

The position of the staircase in the simple block plan is infinitely variable. Sometimes, as at Creevaghmore and numerous early 18th-century examples, it is immediately inside the front door. More often it is at the back, and this is increasingly common towards the end of the century. If there are two staircases, they may be side-by-side at the back,[17] as at Roundwood or Castle Ffrench (14-15, page 173) or one in front of the other, as at Lettybrook or Enniscoe. The staircase is commonly at the side or sides, as at Ledwithstown or Kilduff: sometimes, though rarely, contained in a projecting bow, as at Belview, Co. Meath (87 page 160). Again, if there are two staircases, the main and service staircases may be together at one side, as at Shannongrove, or opposed as at Ledwithstown or Clonbrock.

One very common and persistent position is immediately to the right or left of the front door: that is to say in a compartment forming part of the entrance-front: examples are at Shannongrove, Stewart Lodge, Co. Carlow, Furness, Co. Kildare, Athgoe, Co. Dublin, Dysart, Co. Westmeath and Emsworth, Co. Dublin – that is to say from the very beginning to the very end of the century. It is immaterial whether there is a partition between the hall and the staircase or not. Either way, the result is often that the staircase passes visibly behind a front window, which nobody, including James Gandon, seems to have minded. And why should we?

If the staircase took up a quarter or more of the floor area, as at Furness or Drewstown, we can only conclude that that was the owner's preference: there was good precedent at Ashdown, Berkshire, one of the finest of English Caroline houses. At Sherwood Park the proportion devoted to the staircase is more like one-third: an extreme example. The sense of liberation to those accustomed to winding stone staircases in dark turrets must have been very refreshing.

Halls extending through two storeys are not very common among houses of the size we are mostly considering. The example of Seafield (55-57, pages 109-111) stands almost alone. Roundwood (17-21, pages 124-26) has one, with attractive balconies giving access to the two front bedrooms. Gloster (18-22, pages 86-87), with its two-storey hall opening into an upper hall, is almost too large a house to be in this book at all, though the individual rooms are not very large. At the end of the century, Avondale, Co. Wicklow (Parnell's house) has a splendidly wasteful hall of double height.

There is not a great deal to be said about staircases, which are generally pretty straightforward. Cantilevered stone staircases are generally restricted to the larger houses, though occasionally, as often in the Dublin house, the main staircase is of timber and the service stair of stone: Cooperhill, Co. Sligo is an example. At Kilcoltrim, Co. Carlow the staircase is of stone in a stone box: but mostly they are of timber. One remarkable example is at Woodbrook, Co. Wexford, a spiral 'flying' staircase (1, page 14) somewhat like that of Chevening, a *tour-de-force* of the carpenter's craft, dating from the turn of the century.

The introduction of the bow or polygonal bay, dealt with elsewhere (pages 17–18), makes no real difference to the fundamentals of planning,

1   Free-standing timber staircase of the late 18th century at W O O D B R O O K,
Enniscorthy, Co. Wexford.

though it may and often does make the result more interesting. At the very end of the 18th century, and in the early 19th, the neo-classic phase of planning which takes delight in the ingenious fitting together of *internal* apses, ellipses and so on, in the manner of Robert Adam's Luton Hoo, is a direct importation from England (Lucan House, Mount Kennedy, Castle Coole), and achieves its apotheosis, where smaller houses are concerned, in the unexecuted Gandon design for Carriglas.[18] From this, it is a short step to the Nash school of picturesque assembly of shapes as seen at Gracefield, Co. Laois (a kind of second-hand Nash house). The villas of Sir Richard Morrison (1767–1849) are seldom entirely successful in their external handling, and sometimes, as at Cangort and Bellair, they are downright ungainly, but in their integral decoration and organisation of space they carry us very far from the tradition with which most of this book has been concerned. They have been analysed by Edward McParland.[19]

There are other, isolated, instances of 'geometric' planning which may be mentioned. Most remarkable, perhaps, is the hunting-lodge at Castle Cor, Co. Longford (89, page 161), designed perhaps by Davis Ducart (*floruit circa* 1760-80) and built for Dean Cutts Harman, who died in 1784. It consists of a central octagon, with four central fireplaces back-to-back, and four short two-storey arms radiating from alternate sides of the octagon. The inspiration is clearly from the hunting-lodge at Clemenswerth in Lower Saxony, North-West Germany, by Johan Conrad Schlaun, built between 1737 and 1747. At two subsequent dates perfectly ordinary houses were tacked on to the front of it, one in front of the other, the latter in the twentieth century in tolerably convincing pastiche.

Vernon Mount in County Cork (22–25, pages 176-77) is another house *sui generis*. Based on a combination of ellipse and semicircle, it is an exception to the rule that small houses do not have elaborate upper central lobbies. Indeed, it is an exception to most rules. So is Rath (pronounced Rah) in County Wicklow near Tullow, which has a rather convincingly archaeological porch in antis, leading endwise into an enormous elliptical staircase-hall, so large that only half of it is under the main roof of the house, and the relatively insignificant rooms are on either side of its front half, leaving its back half sticking out in the cold. But this, like other such experiments, adjoins a rather insignificant house of the early 18th century, and is probably an experiment by a learned amateur, probably in about 1800.

Freakish geometry is displayed at Mount Eagle, Killiney, Co. Dublin a house by Sandham Symes junior (*floruit circa* 1840), dated by a model to 1837. It is dramatically sited on a steep rock, and its entrance front faces the sea. The front door is placed, conventionally enough, between two half-octagons, and leads to an axial staircase which divides at the half-landing. But to right and left of the base of the stairs the rooms diverge at 45 degrees, and the outline of the house has, in consequence, triangular salients at the two landward corners. Roofs and stacks follow the 45-degree axes. In a sense, the house looks forward to the so called 'Butterfly-plan' houses of the early 20th century.

The last kick of the 'geometric' manner is perhaps Kingsborough Lodge, Lough Arrow, Co. Sligo, no doubt inspired by its larger neighbour, Nash's Rockingham, but dating, it seems, from as late as the 1850s.

There is another line of development in planning, which is both less freakish and more fruitful than the geometric. This is the use of the half-level or mezzanine arrangement, in which use was made of the obvious fact that, whereas reception-rooms and principal bedrooms need height in proportion to their size, minor rooms can with advantage be quite low. The ingenious solution, of fitting in one more storey in the rere half of the house, was applied as early as the back wing of Ballincar, Co. Sligo in the 17th century,[20] in the 18th century at Summer Grove (26-30, pages 129-33) and elsewhere such as Dowth, Co. Meath, and Kilcoltrim, Co. Carlow, but is commonest in the single-storey houses of the turn of the century, such as Ballygowan Cottage (8, page 194), Fort Shannon (1-2, page 190), Beechlawn, Rathgar (12, page 197), and other houses in the Dublin suburbs, notably those in Waltham Terrace, Blackrock.

Purely single-storey houses make their appearance before the end of the 18th century:[21] inevitably they have about them the air of the 'cultured cottage' if not of the *cottage ornée*. Though the word 'bungalow' appears in English as early as 1676, and, in the form 'Bungalo', is found as a place-name in County Tyrone (a mile east of Irvinestown) before 1900, they were certainly not thought of as 'bungalows' but simply as single-storey houses, but were always outnumbered by the 'top-entry' type of one storey over a basement, as exemplified by Mount Gordon (39, page 136). The role of the basement in Ireland will be dealt with later (see pages 24–26).

BOWS AND ROUND ENDS

THE BOW, WHETHER AT THE FRONT, the back or the sides, or in combination, is so marked a feature of mid-18th-century Irish houses that its ancestry should be enquired into. In English architecture the bow, as distinct from the half-octagon, is a Vanbrughian feature (Blenheim, Castle Howard and several of the Elton Hall sketches), while the half-octagon is Palladian (Isaac Ware's Wrotham Park for example).[22] Sir Edward Pearce was both Vanbrughian and Palladian; yet neither bows nor half-octagons play much part in his extant works nor in his drawings, unless we take the two related buildings of Wardtown and Arch Hall to be his, as they may well be. Yet these bows seem too narrow to suit the role of exemplars.

The enigmatic partly brick building in the bailey of Askeaton Castle fills the bill much better. It has wide semi-circular bows at front and back, and in the front one is a 'Venetian' window on the curve. But we do not know its date. With the bows at each end of Richard Castle's Belvedere of about 1740 and the one at the back of Ballyhaise by the same architect, we are on firmer ground. Ballyhaise is a most remarkable case. Built by Richard Castle (*circa* 1690–1751) in about 1733, it has an *oval* saloon forming a bow in the middle of its back elevation, in the manner of the Palazzo Barberini or Vaux-le-Vicomte. This saloon retains its original plaster decoration on its brick vault. I know of no earlier oval saloon in a house in these islands. We cannot be sure of the date of Newhall, which has fully fledged bows at each end and a half-octagon in the middle. It does, however, seem certain that half-octagons are on the Irish scene as early as in England, and that bows are as soon, and more widely diffused in Ireland than in England, where they make a come-back after Adam. Very shallow bows are, in Ireland as in England, a phenomenon of the very end of the century, whether in front as at Erindale, or at the ends as at Verona, or in the middle as at Ballymore (4, page 191).

It is worth remarking that they are a purely provincial or rural feature, entirely absent from Dublin, though not from Cork. The *backs* of Dublin houses are another matter: at the back they were used to improve the lighting and aspect of the rooms, and usually run full height. It is common for bows in country houses also to run full height – at Stewart Lodge, Co. Carlow even higher – and they are usually given semi-conical roofs, which may have a break at the junction with the main roof, corresponding with the break on plan. At Assolas there is a break in the plan but none in the roof, with the result that the overhang of the eaves is much greater round the bow than it is anywhere else. At Mantua (8–11, pages 120-21) the bow-roofs butted against the end-walls, and inside there were large arches spanning the upper rooms: but the silhouette of the bow-roofs exactly prolonged that of the main roof. At Windy Arbour (19-20, page 175) a superficially similar effect was achieved by different means: here there is only one roof, which has semi-conical terminations and sweeps down behind the parapet. At Dromard (Mount Brown) (59, page 112) the end-bows are only one storey high, and their semi-conical roofs are blunted to accommodate the sills of the first-floor windows. At Ballyowen Cottage (38, page 185) the bows are so shallow as to be in effect sinuosities in the front wall, and the slating is continuously swept, giving a rare and pleasing effect. At Newhall (22-23, page 127) the semi-cones of the end-bows butt against the slope of the main roof, but the central half-octagon has its own balustraded flat. It is, on the whole, rare for end-bows to occur without a break, though, as at Killinane, Co. Carlow, this may be very small. At Belfield (Kilpedder), Co. Wicklow there is no break at all, but this does not make for a very satisfactory design.

Small round-ended cottages exist and have existed: for example that traditionally known as Swift's cottage at Kilroot, Co. Antrim, [23] and another at Chapelizod, Co. Dublin: both now destroyed. Others survive, for example Liskilleen in County Mayo, but it is difficult to determine either their age or their ancestry: to know whether they are – or were – a survival of an older round-ended folk tradition, or a cultural feed-back from the aristocratic tradition, perhaps by way of the *cottage ornée*. Round-ended houses 'of Irish type' are familiar in the early 17th-century military bird's-eye maps. Mr Danaher's opinion[24] is that in the pure folk-tradition any rounded building is rounded only *externally*. but this cannot apply to circular buildings, and it would be impossible to prove that ovals or round-ended rectangles had never existed. It is on the face of it likely that cross-fertilisation did occur, but not probable that it can be proved in any particular instance. Bows without breaks are obviously more likely to be related to the folk-tradition than bows with them.

There are occasional houses with a bow at one end only: Allenstown, Co. Meath, long ago demolished, Drewstown in the same county, and Crannagh, Co. Tipperary (71–72, page 151), where the bow may well be inspired by the pre-existing round mediaeval tower.

MATERIALS

THE VAST MAJORITY OF IRISH HOUSES, like most other Irish buildings down to the middle of the 19th century, are built of rubble stone, the walls varying in thickness from two feet upwards, according to the size of the building. This is easily seen in the case of ruined houses, which are plentiful. A fair amount of brick is used in rear-arches, linings and of course vaulting; but brick as a substantive building material is rare, except in the coastal towns, before the 19th century.

The beauty of exposed brickwork was clearly appreciated at Mount Ievers,[25] Woodlands and Newhall. The way in which brick was used at Eyrecourt and Ledwithstown is all the more surprising. At Eyrecourt (*circa* 1660-70) the whole of the outer walls is of fine red brick on the inner face, laced with continuous bond-timbers at the level of, and forming, the lintels of the windows, while the external face of the walls is of rubble stone rendered with lime-plaster. In much the same way, at Ledwithstown of about 1740, the internal walling and the inner face of the outer walls is of red brick, faced externally with rubble stone and rendering, except for the cut stone dressings. The Eyrecourt technique has some similarities with the construction of buildings of similar date in England, though I do not recall brickwork being faced externally with rubble stone.

It is hard to be sure which is the earliest brickwork in Ireland. A forework in Jacobean style fragmentarily surviving at Blarney Castle, Co. Cork, with superimposed engaged columns, is as likely as any.[26] Jigginstown, Co. Kildare, of about 1637, is probably correctly thought to be the first use of brick on a large scale. It was early used for stacks in buildings otherwise mainly of stone, as at Brazeel, presumably because of its precision and stability in structures of small area such as chimneys. An early instance of brick dressings on a building otherwise of stone is Beaulieu, Co. Louth of *circa* 1665, and there is ample evidence, both in surviving buildings such as the house in the bailey of Askeaton Castle, and in documents[27] (such as No. 146 of the Pearce drawings) that rubble-stone buildings with brick dressings were thought quite acceptable in the early 18th century, however characteristic of 19th-century industrial practice they later became.

Rubbed and gauged brick for window-heads seems always to have been very rare in Ireland: Lisle House, Crumlin,[28] now disappeared, was an example, and probably also Yeomanstown, Co. Kildare (54, page 108), though it is now covered with pebble-dash. In both these buildings the window-heads had undulated arrises characteristic of the Thames valley and eastern England, and found also at Jigginstown. Brick dressings were normally flush, and very probably plastered, as they still are at Crannagh, Co. Tipperary: for the brickwork to be finished proud of the wall-face, as at Beaulieu, is exceptional, but is found at Kildrought House, Celbridge.[29]

Post-mediaeval vaults in Ireland seem always to have been carried out in brick: much superior to stone for this purpose for which the same considerations apply as with stacks. An exception is the structure called the 'Hell-Fire Club' on Montpelier Hill just south of Dublin which is vaulted in stone: its curiously close resemblance to Mount Gordon, Co. Mayo has been noted elsewhere (39, page 136).

Rammed earth was no doubt more widely used for structural walling than is now realised. A rammed-earth building which becomes derelict soon disappears, while one which is well maintained preserves its secret from the casual spectator. The most substantial building known by me to be of rammed earth is Waringstown House, Co. Down, three storeys high; but not long ago I saw a derelict house of some pretension at Balgriffin, Co. Dublin, of very similar construction, and farmhouses and cottages of this material are, or were, legion.[30]

Internal dividing walls, which in the 17th century seem mostly to have been framed partitions – and are so found in Shannongrove – are in the 18th century generally very substantial: more substantial than in most comparable English houses of the period. Usually they are of brick or stone: occasionally turf (peat) is reported, as at Finnebrogue, Co. Down, Hilton, Co. Monaghan, Enniscoe, Co. Mayo, Glin, Co. Limerick and in Dublin City itself.

ROOFS

NOT VERY MUCH IS KNOWN about Irish roofs, at least not by me. Since only one mediaeval Irish roof survives in anything like complete state, all scrupulous modern re-roofings of Irish mediaeval buildings have been based on it. If there ever was an Irish carpentry tradition, it did not survive the 17th century: one finds no such echoes of the mediaeval craft in classical form, such as may be seen in, for example, the Town Hall at Abingdon in Oxfordshire.

A 17th-century roof in reliably original state has yet to be found.[31] By that century the destruction of the forests had caused a serious timber shortage, and by the 18th century the shortage was even worse, except in or near seaports; where good Baltic timber was available, usually under the name of 'Memel fir'. Thus, while the masonry tradition prospered and was strengthened, the carpentry tradition seems to have remained weak. My impression – and for the present it can be no more – is that, building for building, Irish roofs tend to be inferior to their English counterparts.

It is difficult to engage in comparative study because Irish roofs tend to be either inaccessible or not there at all. There is sometimes a short period during which the slates are off but the framing still there to be inspected, and if the stairs are still more or less passable, one may see something: but such opportunities are scattered and fugitive. The great thing is to get there before the ivy. On the other hand, it is common to see a ruined house with three or four courses of slates still in position on the wall-tops, which tells us something about the original form of construction, and is not a spectacle commonly seen in England.

In very general terms, it may be hazarded that Irish roofs tend to have either no principal trusses at all, but only common rafters, or principals hardly to be distinguished from the common kind, and to be short of purlins, or to have purlins of rather slender scantlings. But to this there are numerous exceptions. Athgoe, for instance, has a roof with principals at the appropriate intervals, and purlins of a size which would be expected in a similar English house, and so has Kilmacurragh. Kilduff (9, page 169), on the other hand, has four massive trusses with collars only, thus:

diagonally set spanning from the corners to the stacks, and, between these, nothing but common rafters. As so often, there is a central valley, and of course a secret gutter, that fruitful source of woe.

The fact that in Irish houses the dividing walls are usually so solidly constructed and are carried up to eaves level, and often higher still to form internal gables, makes it of less importance that roof-trusses should be as solid as they must be when required to cover larger spans. Abundance of good stone and of masons, and shortage of large timber, combine towards the same result. This high degree of load-bearing subdivision may be easily studied at, for example, Tudenham (Rochfort), Co. Westmeath, which was unroofed some thirty years ago but still has a tight network of load-bearing walls at the highest level.

Slates are the normal covering: baked tiles are of great rarity, except where brought in by sea, and uncommon even in seaports. Shingles and thatch were used in many buildings which are now slated: often the height of the verge-course reveals that the roof was once thatched. Wilkinson, writing in 1845,[32] speaks of numerous local slate-quarries already disused by this time, and mentions those of Killaloe, Valentia, Benduff near Glandore in County Cork, and Ashford, Co. Wicklow as being still quarried. Shingles and straw, he says, are yielding to slates which are increasingly imported from Wales. He mentions the heavy slates of Mayo, especially those quarried near Westport and already obsolete in his day because of their great weight; and, in the same county, a quartzy sandstone, also very thick and heavy, used for roofs. The heavy Mayo slates are hard to find today. Heathfield, near Ballycastle, Co. Mayo, still has such a roof, but probably not for much longer.

Gutters, other than those worked in the tops of cornices or formed behind blocking-courses or parapets, seem not to have been used. When they have been added later, they usually spoil the profile. Timber cornices are, for climatic reasons, rare, though there were plenty in the 17th century, and plenty again in the 19th. The former have all gone, and the latter are rapidly following them.

STACKS

THE ROLE OF THE STACKS in the plan-form has already been touched upon. A vivid illustration of the difficulty of generalising about 17th-century house plans is afforded by a group of six houses in County Roscommon, five of which are within twenty miles of each other, while the sixth is about twenty miles away.[33] Between them they contain one simple rectangle with stacks at each end, one rectangle with two circular towers at adjacent corners and stacks at each end, one rectangle with an L projection containing a staircase, one rectangle with stacks at each end serving nothing but corner-fireplaces (see Lowberry 1-3, pages 68-69), and with a full-height central projection in front, and two which consist of three blocks set corner-to-corner, making a U-plan, also with end-stacks, four to each house (see Gort, Co. Roscommon 4-5, page 70).

One thing which can be said with some confidence about 17th-century plans is that the stacks tend to be grouped round the periphery of the building, incorporated in the outer walls. This holds good from the grandest examples such as Jigginstown,[34] through the elaborate complexity of Castle Cuffe, Co. Laois which has ten stacks set at right-angles to one another, to the simplest examples such as Dundonnell. To this rule, as to others, Rathfarnham and Portumna Castles[5] are early exceptions, having stacks deep in the centre of the plan, and so is Dromahair, built by Sir Edward Villiers in 1626.

In the next century there was, as already noted, a pronounced tendency in the opposite direction. In a remarkably high proportion of houses the flues are all gathered together into a single stack, or at most into two. Examples are too numerous to mention. In doing this the designers were going clean counter to the advice of John Payne (for whom see pages 51-61), who wrote:

> A Chimney will not carry off the Smoke effectually that is turned round one or more Angles of a Room: for, the Flue being confined to the Thickness of the Walls is too much contracted; and the Contraction of it must in a short time clog it with Soot; and be also a complete Obstacle to its being properly cleaned. Yet this Method is sometimes taken for the Sake of Regularity without-doors. But this Evil we have nothing to do with at present, as it belongs only to great Buildings.

Even when the designers permitted themselves two stacks, regularly disposed, it was sometimes necessary to bring the flues a long way, as in the examples of Dysart or Athgoe (see 35–37, pages 134-35 and 61–63, pages 146-147). In the greatest example of all, Castletown Conolly, it was no small achievement to have gathered all the flues into a mere two stacks. To gather those of a smaller house into one was a good deal easier.

What was the purpose? 'Regularity without-doors' is no doubt part of the answer, perhaps most of it, though two symmetrically arranged chimneys are as regular as one, and more usual. It may be that it was hoped, by leading the gases by such a route, to conserve a higher proportion of the heat within the building. However this may be, it is a frequent enough feature to excite remark. For what it is worth, William Adam and Sir James Clerk did much the same at Mavisbank in Scotland.

The great majority of Irish stacks, whether in town or country, diminish by a sloping offset. This is not unknown in England, but it is much less common there. It is apt to be less in evidence in later houses, such as Emsworth (page 183), where the architect was English: but, left to themselves, Irish builders would normally finish a chimney in this way.

THE BASEMENT

IT IS THE RULE rather than the exception for Irish houses of any size to be raised over a basement: so much so that its absence, as at Kilcarty, or at Frybrook, Co. Roscommon, or at Clonagh, Co. Offaly, is worthy of remark. The basement, whether totally below ground or partly above it, is of course a commonplace of English classical architecture also, but in Ireland it is much more nearly universal. Writing in 1825,[35] C. R. Cockerell attributes its prevalence, and that of the surrounding area, to the necessity of keeping the house dry in 'this wet climate'. The 18th-century Irish basement seems, in fact, to have a triple origin: in an old tradition which was in part at least defensive, in the role of the basement as a kind of damp-course as diagnosed by Cockerell, and of course in the classical basement considered as a plinth, as in Inigo Jones's Queen's House, Coleshill, or Wilton.

The fact that the 10th–12th-century Irish Round Towers are almost invariably entered at first-floor level allows us to regard their ground-floors as defensive basements, and though the typical tower-house-castle of the 15th–17th century is normally entered at ground-floor level, the bottom storey is guard-room and storage space and never treated as more than a prelude to the living-space which begins on the first floor. Some at least of the smaller early 17th-century houses, such as Fennor and Carstown, seem always to have been entered at the level above the basement, though others, such as Castle Baldwin and Brazeel, were entered at ground level.

Even so, there is an excavated half-basement under Castle Baldwin. It was often the case that, though the single doorway might be at ground level, real living took place on the floor above, and the basement windows were minutely small: an excellent example is Killenure, Co. Tipperary.

The two similar grand houses of Kanturk (1609) and Portumna (before 1617) were entered above the basement level, while Strafford's great palace of Jigginstown stands on a high plinth, of which the east half was solid and the west half carried on brick vaulting of the highest quality.

The town-house of Dublin and other major cities, like that of London, had a basement for other reasons, of which the classical exposition was made, once and for all, in Chapter V of Sir John Summerson's *Georgian London*. These reasons are physical and have to do primarily with the making of the finished road-level on a developed estate. In Dublin (by contrast with London) and especially in the Dublin suburbs, there is a marked tendency, after 1800, for the basement to rise progressively out of the ground, until about 1840 it is not an excavation at all, but a full-height storey carrying the principal storey on top of it, so that there may be as many as twenty steps up to the front door.

In the grammar of classical architecture, fully established in Ireland by about 1720 or so, the basement is conceived as a classical plinth upon which stands the order, usually 'notional' rather than expressed by columns or pilasters, but still present in spirit, and regulating the whole elevation. The main entrance may be in the basement itself, as it is at Marble Hill, Twickenham, or at Holkham or at Powerscourt, Co. Wicklow, but it is more likely to be in the *piano nobile*, as it is on the north front of the Queen's House, Greenwich, or as it is in nearly all the Irish houses illustrated here.

While, in the Dublin suburbs, a long flight of steps up to the front door is generally an indication of late date, this does not hold good in the country, as witness Whitewood, Co. Meath, where the front door is reached by a massively monumental flight of steps, or Mount Gordon, Co. Mayo (39, page 136) where the entrance is on the upper of the two floors, though the house is mid-18th-century in style, and, though in a provincial situation, was probably built in the 1770s. Another striking example, though bolder and ruder in execution, is Gaulstown near Castlepollard in County Westmeath (41, page 101).

A fall in the land, as at the Queen's House, Greenwich, must often have been the determining factor. This is apparent at Shannongrove, for example, and accounts for the monumental flight of steps up to the door on the river-front. At Sherwood Park,[17] by contrast, the garden door centrally at the back is at a half-level on the way to the basement. Quite often the 'back' door is at the side and at basement-level, and gives on to a yard. Such is the case at Kilduff (9, page 169), where, surprisingly, the doorcase to the yard is of a formality and grandeur hardly less than that of the front door itself, so that one suspects it to have been brought from elsewhere.

When there is a basement, that is where the kitchen is normally to be found. At Roundwood (17–21, pages 124-26), where the entrance faces east, and the 'back' door is to the north, the kitchen is on the ground-floor at the north-west corner, and there is no basement under the kitchen nor under the room diagonally opposite it, in the south-east corner. But this is unusual: in general, when a house has a basement that basement is co-extensive with the house. The area, which Cockerell remarks upon, is usually treated with a sloping grass bank, but sometimes with a retaining wall, and occasionally, as at Galtrim (39–41, pages 186-87), with a combination of the two.

The practice of connecting the house with outlying offices by a tunnel seems to be peculiar to Ireland, though I have once seen something similar in, I think, West Herefordshire. Strokestown, Bellamont, Castle Coole and Lucan are among the Irish examples. In the nature of things, this is a feature of the grander houses, though it has been reported in connection with some of modest size.[36]

VAULTING

WHILE IT IS NOT EXACTLY COMMON for the ground floors of houses to be vaulted, it occurs often enough to be worthy of remark. Perhaps the earliest example (not including vaulted basements such as Jigginstown) is Rathcoffey, Co. Kildare, which, like Ballyhaise, Co. Cavan by Richard Castle, has the whole of its ground floor vaulted in brick. At Ballyhaise, in fact, the first floor also is vaulted over, while at the King house in Boyle, Co. Roscommon, by one of Pearce's followers, there are, including the basement, no less than four storeys of vaulting one on top of another.

In some ways the most remarkable is Kingsfort (now ruined), Co. Meath, in which three out of the four ground-floor rooms were vaulted in brick to which the remains of mid-century stucco decoration of high quality may still be seen adhering. It is ironical that whereas many hundreds of ceilings on laths have been laboriously and expensively saved, Kingsfort, so much better designed to resist decay and even neglect, should have perished.

In some houses, such as Castlemorres, Co. Kilkenny,[37] vaulting suddenly appears high up in the building where it is least expected: the present state of ruin of Castlemorres has revealed this: the explanation has probably to do with flues and stacks.

Many builders disregarded Payne's advice not to build high in the country ('… it is easy to imagine what a ridiculous and awkward Figure a House of three or four Stories High would make standing alone in an open Field'). Plain farmhouses, in particular, are apt to be three storeys high (see Killininny, 41, page 137, and very many others like it) and often also raised over basements. For a given quantity of accommodation, it is of course true that a cubical house uses the least materials and has the smallest surface area. But it may be doubted that these considerations were uppermost in the minds of the builders: more likely, perhaps, some persistence of the tower-house habit is at work, especially since houses were sometimes built directly on to an existing tower (6, page 71; 4, page 191).

ELEVATIONAL FEATURES

THE MOST WIDELY EMPLOYED elevational feature is, without doubt, the tripartite opening, in one or other of its guises. I prefer to use this term rather than 'Venetian window' because it covers a number of pseudo-Palladian features which, though interrelated, can be distinguished from one another. It should be borne in mind that a round-headed door flanked by side-lights is first cousin to a 'Venetian' window. Such a door occurs in Vanbrugh's Seaton Delaval, where the sidelights are separated from the door by piers of walling, and is repeated in the attic as a tripartite window – or group of windows if one prefers so to consider it. The most obvious parallel to this is at Lismore, and this is one of the reasons for suggesting that Sir Edward Pearce was involved at Lismore. It occurs repeatedly in Pearce's studies, and in his Loughgall designs.[38] It crops up elsewhere; for example, at Newgrove, Knightstown, Holladen, Landsdown, Dromin, Co. Kerry, and, on the curve, at Askeaton. It is prominent in the axial garden-house at Kilmainham which is apparently by Pearce.

Intermediate between this type and the fully orchestrated columnar type of Venetian window comes the type in which the dividing-pier is no wider than a column would be. The tripartite opening on the first storey of the south front of Cuba Court (32–37, pages 94-97) approximates to this type, which is the commonest Irish form in which it occurs.

The third main type which must be distinguished is that in which the central round-headed opening is not in fact an opening, but a niche. The Irish exemplar for this widely used device must be the flanking elevations of Pearce's Bellamont Forest,[39] where he used it to tie together an elevation containing an even number of windows. It is unlikely that Pearce would have done this on a main front, but his successor Richard Castle did, notably at Ballinter and at Nos 119-120 St Stephen's Green, Dublin; and so did Francis Bindon and others. At Dysart, (35-37, pages 134-35) it appears on the main front: but here there is no duality to be resolved.

The fact that the head of the central arch of a Venetian window rises higher than the heads of the flanking windows caused trouble to some designers. It caused trouble to Richard Castle at No. 85 St Stephen's Green, and it embarrassed his follower Francis Bindon, especially at Woodstock, Co. Kilkenny. When there was enough internal head-room, it was reasonable to return the internal cornice on each side of the arch: but when there was not, the temptation was to scale down the Venetian window, with the risk of its appearing too small in relation to the other windows, as happened at Rosemount, Co. Westmeath and Snowhill, Co. Fermanagh. Another solution, adopted at Lissen Hall, Co. Dublin, was to lower the sills of the Venetian windows in relation to those of the adjoining windows, which enabled the Venetian window to hold its own, though at some cost to architectural logic.

Lissen Hall is a particularly interesting example in that it appears to be a remodelling of a plainer house, in obvious emulation of its neighbour 'Mantua' which faced it across the small estuary of the Meadow Water, and, though smaller, was grander in appearance. Whoever remodelled Lissen Hall set out to make it look like Mantua, by adding the curved bows at the ends and a Venetian window in the middle, so lowered that the crown of its arch hardly rises above the heads of the older openings.

The commonest device for giving interest to the centre of a composition was to place a Venetian window above a tripartite door, and a Diocletian window above that, or some variation of this. If the upper elements were kept the same width as the doorcase, the Diocletian window became absurdly large, as at Raford, Co. Galway[40] (perhaps by Francis Bindon). If the width of the upper features was progressively diminished the result was much more pleasing, as at Roundwood, Summer Grove and Dysart, though at the cost of offending against the rule that solid should stand over solid, and void over void. At Mount Juliet, Co. Kilkenny the nearly identical features become narrower in an almost mechanical manner. The designer of Newgrove, Co. Meath found an ingenious method of overcoming the difficulty, but it does not seem to have been widely copied. In a purely two-storey context, at Colganstown and Newberry, Nathaniel Clements[41] (1705-77) showed himself able to manage the matter with some grace (77, page 154).

Most Irish owners could not afford porticoes. Indeed there is not much evidence that they wanted them. They are rare in the early 18th century – among larger houses Bellamont, and among smaller Seafield (55, page 109) – but not many more, and they return again in the early 19th, as at Upton, Co. Carlow or Hermitage (St Enda's), Co. Dublin. They are a little commoner in the larger houses, where they strike an operatic note, especially in ruin or decay as at Mount Shannon, Co. Limerick or Kenure, Co. Dublin: both by English architects. But the mood of Irish architecture is more often elegaic, and the elegaic note is dominant in such an example as Annesbrook (16–17, page 200).

When external adornment is precluded by poverty, prudence or puritanism (architectural or other), there are other ways of giving interest to an elevation. One of these is by the spacing of the windows, and this was widely used by the Irish designers. To some extent, of course, such spacing is dictated, or at least suggested, by the plan-form. This is obviously so at Piedmont (47-49, page 105) where the result is to slow up the rhythm in the centre, and at Carnmeen (38, page 136) where it has the opposite effect. Whether the essentially similar, though more sophisticated result at Prior

Park (21, page 176) arises purely from such causes or in part from sources such as the plate in Book VII of Sebastiano Serlio's *Tutte l'Opere d' Architettura* and its numerous derivatives, is a very open question, and one, furthermore, which seems to me not to be worth trying to answer.

The truth is, surely, that the designers and craftsmen of the period were so deeply imbued with the language of classicism, and that it answered so well to their everyday needs, that they used it unselfconsciously and felt no need to be scurrying off continually to look things up in pattern-books. It was thus that the simple gable-ended, 'Palladian'-centred farmhouses repre-sented here by Streamstown (76, page 153), Cloon (74, page 152) or Clonbrogan (75, page 153), came to be as they are. And for the same reasons the feature of the Colganstown doorcase which gives it life and individu-ality – the touch of lyrical fancy in the glazing – is precisely that which does not come from any of the pattern-books.

It has already been noted that in the early period there is a tendency, persistent rather than pervasive, to group the windows together towards the centre of the façade, leaving a wide mass of masonry at the corners. It is very marked at Graney in the 17th century, and at Piedmont, Tober, Yeomanstown, Cooperhill, Port Hall and Lissenhall: all, except perhaps for the last, in the first half of the century. It seems to me to indicate an aesthetic preference (and one, by the way, not always uppermost in the mind of Palladio – see the villas Godi and Malcontenta); but there may be some overtones of defence and structural stability in operation as well.

Whether the windows are grouped or not, the expedient of the 'floating' pediment or pediment-gable was a popular device for holding a façade together. I call a pediment 'floating' when it is not accompanied by an outward break, and more particularly when it disregards the openings in the wall below. Corbally (10, page 80) is a typical instance, and Athgoe (63, page 147) is another. Floating pediments, especially where, as at Athgoe, they are steeply pitched, are a universal mark of provincialism. Even where the pediment rests correctly on a breakfront, uncertainty of handling may bring the openings uncomfortably near to the external corner, as may be seen at Allenton (14, page 83). But on the whole it is remarkable how free country architecture soon became of such solecisms. The builders, like M. Jourdain, were speaking good prose without knowing it.

Like causes produce like effects, and it is not surprising that there are, in Scotland, some houses, such as Airds, Glendoich and Duchal, which at a casual glance could be mistaken for Irish houses. It has been shown[42] that the Irish designers used the plates of William Adam the elder, current from 1720 onwards, though not in the collected form as *Vitruvicus Scoticus* until 1810, as a mine from which to quarry themes and compositions. But these houses in Scotland, and their counterparts in Ireland, resemble each other much more than either of them resembles the Adam plates. Irish buildings of the period not only are solid; they have also, and very markedly, the appearance of solidity; climate, geology, economics and temperament were to ensure that this would hold good right down to the frontiers of the vernacular manner, and beyond.

WINGS

FOR MANY PEOPLE THE COUNTRY-HOUSE with wings is the very embodiment of the 18th century, and the popular stereotype is that of the wings linked to the house by quadrant colonnades. The concave quadrant (by which the wings are advanced) is in fact only one of many variants, and not the commonest, while the colonnade is decidedly rare. Among greater houses, the straight arcade is the favourite of Davis Ducart,[43] while straight colonnades were preferred in the neo-classic from 1780 onwards, as at Lyons, Castle Coole and the remodelling of Carton.

There is a typological sequence in the matter of wings, but to attempt to give the chronological order, and to identify the types at the same time, would lead only to bewildering confusion. It seems best, therefore, to begin with types which appear early in the record (even if they are also very persistent), and to go on to arrangements which are mainly or wholly of later occurrence.

The 'deep courtyard' plan, in which the wings face one another and form, with the house, a hollow square open at the front, is found throughout Europe. An early, and humble, Irish example is Milk Park, Co. Carlow. A grander example at Holly Hill, Co. Cork, on the Bandon river, is known from a drawing in the Kinsale Museum, and not far away, at Garrettstown (45, page 104), the two wings survive of a house which, itself, may never have been built: instead, one of the wings was enlarged to form the house. At Mount Merrion, Co. Dublin the surviving, rather modest, house seems to have been one of three blocks arranged in this fashion. At Springhill, Co. Derry (88, page 160) long service blocks face one another across the approach, and at Port Hall, Co. Donegal there is a similar arrangement, though at the 'back' of the house, facing the river Foyle. The modest agricultural layout at Ballynure, Co. Wicklow (10, page 170), though late in date, embodies the same idea, and, for all its formality, is visibly and functionally a farmyard.

The type of small cubical wing, usually lower than the house, which stands advanced from the main block at each end, and overlaps it by the thickness of one wall which is common to both house and wing, has a long history. It resembles the musical device in which the last note of one phrase is the first note of the next. In plan, if not in silhouette, it appears as early as Jigginstown (1637), and by the time of Waringstown, Co. Down it is fully established. Buncrana,[44] Co. Donegal (6-7, page 79), though sharply contrasted in other ways, is an example from the very early 18th century. Lismore Castle, probably from about 1730, has it also, and so has Dunmore, Co. Laois (near Durrow, now a shell). It appears again at Emsworth (34–36, pages 182-83), in Francis Johnston's Phoenix Park design (11, page 196) and as late as the 1830s in an unimportant design by an unimportant architect, now in the National Library.

This 'overlapping wing' seems at first sight to have something to do with the early 17th-century arrangement exemplified at Gort and Athleague, Co. Roscommon (4, 5, page 70). Yet I think there is an essential difference, in that in the County Roscommon examples the wings are not only the same height as the house, but overlap it by a wide enough margin to accommodate a communicating doorway. They approximate, in fact, to the U-plan, and have probably a more than casual eye to defensive advantage.

The question of what these and other wings were used for is emphatically secondary to the question of their form, however unpalatable this may be to a certain school of thought. So far from form following function, it is well-nigh the other way about: in large establishments the wings, whether detached or conjugate, are used for kitchens, stables and the like, while in small establishments they are barns and byres. In formal terms they are autonomous, and are put there for sculptural reasons.

There is a kind of L-shaped wing which appears early and seems to have a wide, though sparse, distribution. The examples at Shannongrove (3, page 76) and Lismore (23, page 88) are in essence strikingly similar, and not the least of their similarities is that initially both pairs appear to have had curvilinear gables. Those at Lismore which face the house (and hence do not show on the elevation) are still curvilinear, and the end gables have probably been simplified in rebuilding. Springhill, Co. Derry, again, provides a parallel (88, page 160). The curvilinear gable was once widespread on houses also, but survivors are now very rare.

The pavilion-wings connected by curved sweeps have already been mentioned. Those at Old Carton were the first in Ireland: those at Castletown Conolly are the earliest surviving, and incomparably the most splendid. In humbler examples, a plain curved wall takes the place of the colonnade. An example of a really very small house with such wings is Belview, Co. Meath (87, page 160); an example of a not very pretentious house linked by curved walls to large barns acting as wings is Springhill, Co. Laois (68-69, page 149). At Landenstown (42, page 138) the large barn-wings are articulated with small but effective changes of plane, and linked to the house by canted archways. Sometimes the curved sweeps are convex, as at Moone, Co. Kildare, and sometimes they sweep *back* from the house: but the consideration of these must wait for that of the 'economic layout' with which they are so often linked.

An obvious expedient to take the 'boxiness' off a simple cube is to add, as part of the design, or later, single-storey flanking extensions in the same plane as the front. As might be expected, this is fairly common. Another example is Beechwood, near Nenagh, Co. Tipperary. Kilcarty is a later instance, of a rather special kind (see pages 164-66), and Galtrim and Ballynagall, Co. Westmeath, both by Francis Johnston, are later still, one markedly more successful than the other. In almost every case such wings are two windows wide, and this seems to be the right number. At Kilcarty the wing windows are square and the same size as the upper windows of the main block (2, page 165).

An unexpectedly large number of houses have detached utilitarian wings faced – usually in blind though not always – with some form of 'Palladian' feature: usually the 'Venetian' window or some variant of it. More often than not such wings have been mutilated or partly destroyed for conversion into tractor-sheds and the like, and sometimes one is missing altogether, though its former existence can be traced on the 1829–42 Ordnance Survey. Aghaboe (58, page 112) was formerly flanked by a pair of such wings: one has disappeared and the other is now just visible to the eye of faith.

The wings at Aghaboe were, not very effectively, right up against the house. Much more commonly they are detached, or linked by plain walls with wickets or piered openings. Among the grander houses, Altavilla, Co. Limerick, has wings, each with two pairs of window-flanked niches, a trope absent from the house itself. Similarly – and perhaps more typically – the detached pavilions at Sherwood Park (46-47, page 140) have similar motifs, singly, and entirely in blind. Other very typical instances are at Ballyraheen, Co. Wicklow, Youngstown, Co. Kildare, Johnstown, Co. Kildare (near Enfield), Crosshaven, Co. Cork, probably also Odelville, Co. Limerick, Annsgift, Co. Tipperary, and no doubt many more. The little pavilion at Lisdonagh, Headford, Co. Galway (31-33, page 181) belongs to this class, though it is doubtful whether its companion was ever built.

The early 18th-century house at Haystown, Co. Dublin, has continuous straightly extended wings more in the Vanbrugh than in the 'Palladian' manner, but, so far at least, this seems to be on its own. Also on its own is the 45-degree arrangement found at Milcum, Co. Mayo.

A graceful, if not very numerous, class of wings (if so they can be properly called) consists of those best described as 'lean-tos' in as much as they are visibly in that form. Mount Gordon, Co. Mayo (39, page 136) and Erindale, Co. Carlow (5, page 192) are here illustrated: other instances are the so-called 'Hell-Fire Club' in the Dublin mountains, and Orchardton, Templeogue, Co. Dublin. The lean-to may be either a straight sloping line or an S-curve.

Lastly, and perhaps of greatest interest, comes the type of wing in which a subsidiary building is presented end-on to the spectator. This is quite distinct from the 'deep courtyard' type: we are now concerned with complexes in which the enclosed space is behind the house, not in front of it. This can best be considered together with the 'economic layout'.

As the Knight of Glin has made clear,[45] the incorporation of the farm-buildings into an architectural composition with the house was not only practised by Palladio in his Veneto villas, but enjoined upon his English followers by Isaac Ware (1735 ?) in *A Complete Body of Architecture*:

> The plan may be so made that ... it may appear much more considerable to the eye. The barn may now be a detached building ... and the stable and

cart-house, answered by the cow-house, separated from the principal building only by a gate on each side, may stand as two wings; which, with very little decoration from a judicious builder, will have a pretty effect.

– words which, in Ware's own country, seem to have fallen on deaf ears, since Palladian farm-complexes, or 'economic layouts', are not reported from England. Whether the idea of placing a large square farmyard axially immediately behind the house was inspired by Ware or arose spontaneously is not easy to say. It is a fairly obvious idea, after all, and at Creevaghmore, for example (49–50, pages 141-42), where it occurs, there is no attempt to dress up the farm-buildings, and the house (apart from its curiously close resemblance to one of Payne's ground-plans) does not have the air of having been taken from a pattern-book. At Clonmaskill, Co. Westmeath the farm-buildings do not match one another, but their gables appear flanking the house in a more or less balanced way. At Edenmore, Co. Donegal (11, page 170) they present polygonal ends flanking the house, giving an effect much like the inner wings at Springhill in the neighbouring county of Derry. At Inch, near Balbriggan in north County Dublin, they have hipped ends and are joined to the house by short walls containing niches. At Clooncallick, Co. Fermanagh, low convex quadrant ranges sweep back from the house to the farm-buildings whose gabled-ends have some degree of formality.

The type, in short, is well-established and widespread. In its more elaborate form, with five harmonised and contrasted elements strung out in a row, it is especially associated with the counties of Dublin, Kildare and Meath, and the Knight of Glin has shown reason[45] to connect it with the name of Nathaniel Clements (1705-77). He has also shown that Clements, like other Irish architects, made use of themes (such as the Colganstown pavilions) drawn from the published designs of William Adam the elder (1689-1748). The finished article, however, has a very different flavour and feeling from either Adam's engravings or his executed work.

The most important of Clements's economic layouts are Colganstown, Co. Dublin (77-82, pages 154-58), Williamstown, Co. Kildare, Belview, Co. Meath, perhaps Newberry, Co. Kildare, and Lodge Park, Co. Kildare. At Colganstown and Williamstown, in particular, great play is made with advance and recession by quadrant-walls, though the wings themselves have fronts all on the same plane. Nathaniel Clements was an eclectic architect in the sense that he picked and chose his elements from pattern-books and combined them so that they compose well enough together; but they do not interact on one another. It would be easy to substitute the pavilions from one another, and they would look much the same. In fact, the same elevation was used twice over, at Colganstown and Newberry, with hardly any change, but whether Clements's hand was at work on both occasions seems to me increasingly open to question.

There is one economic layout which is of a different order altogether from any of Clements's: one which satisfies the requirement of the late A. E. Richardson that 'real architecture requires to be molten in the imagination of the designer',[46] and that is Kilcarty by Thomas Ivory of Dublin (*circa* 1720-86), of which an analysis will be found on page 164.

There is a clear relationship between the economic layouts and the series of 'model farms' for Marley, Co. Louth, designed by Francis Johnston for Archbishop Robinson in 1793.[47] These, in turn, are closely paralleled in the executed Church Hill model farm at Ballykelly, Co. Derry, built in 1824 by the London Fishmongers' Company.[48] The difference is that in both these cases a landlord intended the enterprise to be occupied by a tenant, whereas in the Colganstown and Kilcarty types the owner is the occupier. But the role of the wings is the same, which is the essential point.

Before leaving the subject of wings, we should mention the totally detached type, such as the 'ink-pot' wings at Belline, Co. Kilkenny, of which one was designed as a dovecote. The considerably earlier, but equally vertical, tower-wings at Dollardstown were of unknown purpose: indeed, it seems that no final decision was ever taken as to what purpose they should be adapted to serve.

DOORCASES

THERE IS NOT, all things considered, as much variety in country house doorcases as might have been expected. In the early period this may not have been so: the timber doorcases at Eyrecourt and Kilmacurragh, one now completely gone though known from photographs, and the other already incomplete, suggest a wider range of variation than is now observable. In Dublin itself there must have been somewhat more variety than there is now, especially during the period when timber was widely employed. The Ardee Street doorcase[49] was probably not exceptional. Bolection mouldings, so common in England, seem always to have been very rare in Ireland. There are two bolection-moulded doorcases in the old meeting-house in Eustace Street, and there was one at the City Bason (now re-erected at Leixlip Castle); but in the provinces I have recorded only Randalstown, Co. Meath, Castle Martin, Co. Kildare (4, page 39) and the Mayoralty House in Galway.

The vast majority of doorcases are made of stone, and the stone is usually the local limestone. The pattern and detail are generally such as would have been found in Dublin at the same date or a little earlier. The doorcases of, for example, Athgoe, Co. Dublin, Kilduff, Co. Offaly, Prior Park, Co. Tipperary and Leslie Hill, Co. Antrim are straight out of the pattern-books and without solecisms. Rockmount, Co. Galway and Scregg, Co. Roscommon, have doorcases with charmingly wayward detail, the result no doubt of some degree of ignorance. Those of Shannongrove and Mountainstown have a Baroque exuberance not now to be found in the capital, if it ever was; and a similar feeling characterises the west door of the disused church of Durrow, Co. Offaly of about 1700. The Platten and Castle Martin doorcases are of great splendour, as is that of Santry Court (intended to be re-erected in Dublin Castle), but apart from the use at Castle Martin of a bolection-moulding as already noted, they are in no way extraordinary in terms of design.

Occasionally there is a departure from the grammar of ornament as practised in the capital, as, for example, at Lissanisky, Co. Tipperary (7, page 41) or Davidstown, Co. Kildare. The motive often seems to be the desire to get a wider and larger fanlight so as to light a hall which, in the country, was generally larger than that of a town-house, and much more continually in use. The result is often the omission or elision of elements which by strict logic ought to be present. Provincial doorcases are apt to lack frieze or cornice: in very extreme cases they may lack even an architrave. An amusing example of the naive combination of elements, each in themselves elegantly formed and decorated, is to be seen in 8, page 41 at Philipstown, Co. Offaly. Another doorcase, remarkable for its scale, is to be seen at Portarlington (10, page 43) and is equally unlike anything in Dublin. Someone had presumably read his Vignola, or just possibly seen Caprarola,

2

2   Doorcase at PLATTEN HALL, Donore, Co. Meath. The glazing of the fanlight resembles that in the north courtyard doorway into the hall of the Royal Hospital Kilmainham, and the flanking windows are of Dublin Castle type. The house was probably of about 1700, and possibly by Sir William Robinson (*floruit* 1670-1712). It had a large hall with an open-well staircase, and much panelling, and was demolished in the mid-1980s. The green marble lions survive.

3

3 A fine scroll–pediment doorcase of
1710 at B A L L Y M A C H R E E S E,
Ballyneety, Co. Limerick. The remarkable, perhaps unique, 'petal' steps have
now been dismantled and broken up.

4 Doorcase at C A S T L E M A R T I N,
Kilcullen, Co. Kildare. It is common
for the front doors of country houses
(but not of Dublin houses) to be of
the two-leaf type, as here. The bolection moulding seen here is very rare
in Ireland and the date must be
before 1730, perhaps before 1720.

4

5

5 Detail of the doorcase at
WATERSTON, Co.
Westmeath, built about 1749 by
the German-born architect and
military engineer Richard Castle
(*circa* 1690–1751).

6 MILCUM or MELCOMBE,
Newport, Co. Mayo: note the
provincial omission of the architrave and frieze. The house has
small detached wings set at forty-
five degrees to the main block.

6

7

8

7 Doorcase of unusual and not entirely satisfactory design at LISSANISKY, Nenagh, Co. Tipperary. The monolithic mullions and lintels are of a common occurrence, but they are out of scale with the large voussoirs over the fanlight.

8 A late 18th-century doorcase at PHILIPSTOWN, Co. Offaly. Note the absence of architrave and cornice, except for the 'cornice' on top of the keystone. Decorated keystones are a local feature.

9

9   Admirable masonry and a particularly delicate fanlight at B I R R , Co. Offaly, a house of
about 1815 in Oxmantown Mall.

10 Doorcase, probably early 19th century, in Portarlington at the house called THE DEANERY. What would otherwise be an ordinary enough round-headed doorcase has here been framed in a composition lifted from Giacomo Barozzi da Vignola's *Regole delle Cinque Ordini d'Architettura* and used by him at Caprarola. The 'disappearing' pilaster and impost-moulding come from there, and so does the entablature, Farnese lilies and all, though it has become curiously shrunken in transit.

11 Inner fanlight-guard of wrought iron at MOUNT HANOVER, Duleek, Co. Meath, an early 18th-century house noted for its fine ironwork. See also 61, page 114.

11

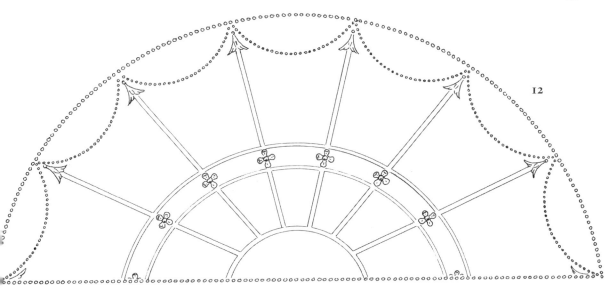

12

12 Fanlight (now in a house in Dublin) of zinc or pewter, with cast-lead enrichments, from DOOLISTOWN, Trim, Co. Meath.

though the Mannerist trick of the 'disappearing pilaster' may be seen in St Mark's Church, Dublin, of about 1727. This Portarlington doorway is probably nearly a century later.

Although direct evidence is lacking, it seems that doorcases were generally dressed and carved on site rather than being supplied from masons' yards in Dublin or provincial centres. In some cases this is doubtful: for example at Sherwood Park, where the coursing of the ashlar walling and the coigns is to a larger module than that of the doorcase itself, which would hardly have happened, one supposes, had the same masons been working on both in the same place. At Lissenhall, on the other hand (43-44, page 139) the module for the coigns and the doorcase is different and all the work was clearly carried out *in situ* and in the same stone. The Limerick Custom House is an interesting example. Though not a country house, it is a similar building, by a country-house architect (Ducart) in a provincial situation; and what is true of it is *a fortiori* likely to be true of some country houses. At Limerick the capitals of the giant pilasters are an inch or two too narrow for their function, which can only have been an error of mensuration. From surviving remains at quarry-sites,[50] we know that, at least in the 19th century, capitals were fully finished at the quarry, with all the risks, physical and other, which that entailed.

Such buildings as Cuffesborough, Co. Laois or Williamstown, Co. Meath may be rather dull and gaunt as designs, but their doorcases are, in design and execution, fully up to the best Dublin standards.

THE CORNICE

IRISH ARCHITECTS WERE PERFECTLY CAPABLE of profiling cornices, and Irish masons of executing them, as countless examples show. They seem, nevertheless, to have been rather reluctant to use the cornice when they could get away with a plain coping instead. Perhaps they were taking their cue from Dublin, where the plain 4.5 to 6 inch coping is the rule, to finish a parapet, eaves being forbidden in the capital. At Dysart (35-37, pages 134-35) for example, a whole pediment is so defined, and the moulding used at Millmount (65-67, page 148) can only just by courtesy be called a cornice at all. Both Piedmont and Cuba Court, in their sharply contrasted ways, are early buildings with cornices correctly deployed. Yet in Sir Richard Morrison's design No. 2 in his book of 1793, a 6-inch coping-type 'cornice' is clearly indicated in the drawings, and Gandon's Emo Inn, as erected, has the same feature.

What is the reason for this? It cannot be ignorance, since the buildings in question are otherwise free from solecisms. This is admittedly not always so: at Ballysallagh, for example (60, page 113), it does appear that the builder did not really understand about cornices. Yet often the key must be sought in the architect's intentions. Nearly all Sir Edward Pearce's surviving drawings show buildings with full cornices, but by no means all of Vanbrugh's do: and he, at least, clearly envisaged pediments as simply profiled as that of Dysart.[51]

Of course it costs less to finish a wall-top in this simple manner than to give it a full cornice, but I doubt very much if this is the whole story. It does not cost less to *draw* a full cornice. When Morrison drew a simple 6-inch square moulding, we can only suppose that he intended it. Unfortunately we have no drawings by Nathaniel Clements or by any other of the architects whom we presume to have designed the minor houses which are the subject of this book. We do know that it was part of Thomas Ivory's duty as Master of the Dublin Society's School of Architectural Drawing to produce farmhouse designs[52] and one Ivory design for a small house survives in the collection at Castle Coole. Nor have we much information on what degree of supervision there was, and how responsibility for design details was divided. The Irish reluctance to use the cornice is a stubborn fact, and, at least for the present, must be left as one.

DETAILS

SOME OF THE SIGNIFICANT DIFFERENCES between Irish building practice and that of England remain to be mentioned. The oak sill which rests on the stone sill, and on which the lower and inner sash rests when closed, is in England normally extended to form a housing for the bottom of the part of the frame in which the outer and upper sash slides, whereas in Ireland it is under the lower sash only and is called the 'half-sill'. The result is to leave the end-grain of the outer sash-guide butting against the stone sill and vulnerable to rot. In this matter English practice seems to be clearly superior to Irish. Very occasionally the upper sash is made to disappear completely into a slot in the wall above the window: I know of instances from County Roscommon and County Armagh, but the practice does not seem to be widespread.

In Ireland the front doorstep is always in the same plane as the outer surface of the door, which is fitted with a hinged flap on rollers, which, when the door is closed, drops down over the junction between door and sill and forms an effective seal against the weather. This admirable device does not seem to be known in England: its connection with the Irish climate is obvious.

Less obvious is the reason for the absence of door-saddles from England. They are fitted in Ireland between the jambs of internal doors and are, on plan, about three times as wide as the door is thick. In section they are this shape:

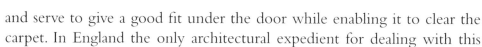

and serve to give a good fit under the door while enabling it to clear the carpet. In England the only architectural expedient for dealing with this problem is the rising hinge: elegant but expensive.

The eleven-panelled door, which is three panels wide except for the bottom row which is divided into two, appears to be unknown or very rare indeed in England, where doors are usually made two panels wide. The Irish method in which part of the door is divided into two and part into three panels, seems both structurally and aesthetically preferable, though more expensive.

Extravagance is the hallmark of the locks so often found on the insides of these front doors (13, page 47). The cases were usually made by hollowing out most of a solid slab of mahogany to make a casing for the steel lock which is inserted from behind, while the front is garnished with handsome brass mountings, escutcheon and drop-handle. They appear to have been made mostly in Dublin, but at least one is known with the signature of a Limerick maker.

13 Typical Irish front-door lock of the mahogany dug-out type with brass mountings, found in countless houses both in Dublin and in the country, apparently from the middle of the 18th century onwards. They were made in Limerick as well as in Dublin, and perhaps also in other centres. They are now much coveted and tend to be moved from house to house. This one is not in its original situation, but many others no doubt are, for example; at DYSART, Delvin, Co. Westmeath which has one very similar to this.

In many Irish houses there is a charming detail which I have never noticed in an English house. The shutter-cases are usually canted, as they are in England; but so, often, is the boxed-in lintel above them, and the resulting triangular space is filled with a pleasant reeded or fluted fan, which in the best work (for example at Kilcarty) is shaped like a segment of a hollow cone. In cheaper work it is flat, but still radially fluted or reeded, as in the room in which these words are being written.

DISTRIBUTION AND ASPECT

THE GEOGRAPHICAL DISTRIBUTION of middle-sized houses is of some interest. Clearly, the figures on which my generalisations are based must be subjective: they are no more than the numbers of houses which have, for one reason or another, engaged my attention: about four times as many as are mentioned in this book. I can only plead that they have not been cooked; for what they are worth, they have emerged of their own accord.

If the counties with the highest numbers of such houses are tabulated, without correction for the differing areas of the counties, the nine counties with the highest scores are Dublin, Tipperary, Meath, Cork, Limerick, Kildare, Laois, Offaly and Westmeath. On the map they form a continuous unbroken belt stretching from Dublin to Meath at the north-east to Cork-Limerick at the south-west. 'Cork' for this purpose means the county east of a line from, say, Rosscarbery to Millstreet. Lest it be thought that this result is greatly influenced by differing rates of survival in different counties and by the limits of my personal experience, I can only say that though there is no doubt such an effect, I believe it to be rather small.

There are significant numbers of interesting houses in Donegal, east Galway and Down (the first two very large counties, the last of average size but more than average population, then as now) but in absolute numbers they fall short of those in the belt already identified. The most surprising conclusion to emerge is the relative poverty of the south-east, particularly Wexford, Waterford and Kilkenny. One might have expected that those long-settled and prosperous river-valleys of the Slaney, the Nore and the Barrow would have had more to show. But surprisingly it is not so. Perhaps the widespread destruction which the Ninety-Eight Rising brought to Wexford has something to do with it. In recent years County Kilkenny has had an unenviable record of destruction of minor houses: I do not know why. In 1783 it had three times as many subscribers to Taylor and Skinner's *Maps of the Roads of Ireland* as County Kildare.[53]

On the positive side, it is not difficult to see why the rich agricultural and pastoral belt stretching from Drogheda to Limerick should have preeminence in this respect. Naturally, also, the small county of Dublin has a score out of all proportion to its area.

Nearly all the houses in question are in lowland areas. Our predecessors did not care much for mountains, and, practical considerations apart, preferred to enjoy them at a distance. Even to come on such a house as Ballysallagh above the 300-feet contour is mildly surprising.

In the matter of aspect no very clear pattern can be discerned. Popular belief would have it that the 18th-century builders perversely always made their houses face north. Analysis of the aspect of several hundred houses gives small support to this view. It is true that sunlight was, rightly, regarded as harmful to upholstery and to books, nor was its effect on the human skin esteemed until very recently. It is, perhaps, just possible to detect a preference for an east-west aspect as recommended by John Payne, but this is by no means decisive. For example, the principal room of Colganstown has windows to north (one), west (two) and south (one).

A good view, on the other hand, was prized, at least from the middle of the 18th century onwards.

> As the shortest and most commodious Approach to a House is always to be chosen, it may so happen that a Town, Wood, Lake or River may lie off the End of your House; and then such a Return as this will command the desired Prospect ….

It is characteristic of the temperate outlook of the period that a view of a town is regarded by Payne as equally desirable with that of a lake, wood or river. Many owners disregarded Payne's advice to keep the drive as short as possible, and went to the other extreme, especially in some of the Midland counties. The drives of County Longford seem to be the longest, nor is this merely the effect of their being so very full of holes: measurement on the map confirms the impression.

GLEBE‑HOUSES

THE GLEBE-HOUSES of the (formerly established) Church of Ireland are an important category of house, because of their ubiquity, their charm, and the influence which they undoubtedly had on other buildings.

According to Donald Akenson, following Daniel Augustus Beaufort's *Memoir of a Map of Ireland*,[54] there were only 354 glebe-houses in existence in 1787 (that is barely more than ten per county),[55] and 829 in 1832. Elsewhere he says that during the first thirty years of the 19th century 550 glebe-houses were built. The discrepancy (between 475 and 550) no doubt represents the number of existing glebe-houses replaced during the period. This programme was in large part financed by Parliament – first the Irish Parliament, after 1800 that of the United Kingdom – through the Board of First Fruits, and went *pari passu* with a programme of church-building. By 1780 the Board (founded in 1711) had built 45 glebe-houses, and between 1791 and 1803, 116, a considerable acceleration of output. The years of greatest government assistance (£60,000 per annum) were 1810-1816 inclusive. Some of this, of course was spent on churches, but a comparable amount (in the proportion of three to four) went on house-building.

During much of this period John Bowden is given in the Directories as 'architect' to the Board. But it is not to be supposed that he personally designed all or most of them. Indeed we know for certain that Francis Johnston, for example, did some,[56] and there were doubtless many architects involved. Though the glebes have a family resemblance, they are not uniform. The Reverend John Payne designed that at Trim, which in its present form is externally rather dull, and a good deal earlier than most.

The characteristic glebe-house is a two-storey, three-bay house with a basement, a hipped roof and either two stacks or a single stack, well set about with trees and with a yard at the back. They set the tone for many another decent-sized and comfortable house, and it is by no means easy to tell whether a house was a glebe-house or not without looking at the older Ordnance Survey maps. For the most part the glebe-houses have been sold off by the church authorities and are now in the hands of lay occupants, and are are worthy of suitable size for modern needs. They have thus tended to survive. They are common everywhere, but there was a particular increase during the early 19th century in the dioceses corresponding to the counties of Meath, Westmeath, Offaly, Wexford, Carlow, Laois, Clare, Longford, Down, Antrim and Louth. Occasionally, as at Aghaboe, Co. Laois, the windows are recessed within arches, or there is some other such refinement, but for the most part they are very simple, very appropriate, and very well built. An example with a little more pretension than most, and from a somewhat earlier date, is Dromiskin (70, page 150) which there is some reason to think may have been designed by the Reverend John Payne.

THE PATTERN-BOOKS OF JOHN PAYNE AND HIS CONTEMPORARIES

REMARKABLY FEW ARCHITECTURAL BOOKS were published in 18th-century Ireland, and the few that were are concentrated in the 1750s. Two large manuscripts by Michael Wills from this period survive but were never published. The large book by John Aheron was in manuscript by 1751 and in print by 1754: though the book was published in Dublin, his practice seems to have lain mainly in the south.

There is no doubt that the pattern-books of James Gibbs and Isaac Ware, the published plates of William Adam, and of course the practice of Pearce and Castle provided most of the vocabulary of the practitioners of the mid-century, including Aheron himself. As early as 1727, and as far away as Wisbech in Cambridgeshire, the garden front of Peckover House displays the combination of tripartite doorcase, surmounted by a Venetian window, surmounted in turn by a Diocletian window, which was to become so very familiar in Ireland.

But these are the surface trimmings of architecture. A closer insight into the marrow of small country-house building is afforded by a deceptively simple-seeming little work, the Reverend John Payne's *Twelve Designs for Country Houses*, the manuscript of which is dated 1753, and the printed version 1757. Payne was born in Dublin in 1700, the son of a portrait painter, and is said to have been an accomplished painter himself. As well as the book on small houses, he wrote another on 'Ornamental Architecture' which was not published and seems to have disappeared. He was incumbent of Castlerickard, Co. Meath, and died in Dublin in 1771. At least one other copy of his designs exists, in the State Paper Office. He has his feet firmly on the ground, and though technically an amateur in that his motive was 'the certain Pleasure he took in doing it', there is nothing amateurish either about his approach to architectural problems, or about his ability to draw. He starts off with the correct specifications of lime and sand for mortar, and devotes two pages to this all-important subject before going on to that of chimneys and how to ensure that they draw properly. On this subject we have already heard him.

There is not room for more than one set of stairs in a small house. A dry area round a house will keep it from damp. The fewer valleys in a roof, the better. Skimping on lead is false economy. Roofs in the Irish climate need a slope of 42.5 degrees. Houses in the country should be as low as possible. Let the principal front of the house face east, never north or south. It is better to have no cornice than a wooden one (the Irish climate again!). And so on, all in a very practical vein indeed.

Payne disarms the criticism that he has said nothing about cost by observing that costs vary so much from place to place that it would be of no use, and besides, everyone knows that not one building in fifty is finished within the estimate.

We know of only one house actually designed by Payne: the glebe-house at Trim, the elevation of which resembles Corbally, Co. Kildare (10, page 80). It is a simple gable-ended house with end-stacks and a simple entrance-and-staircase hall. It was built in 1751 but given a much duller front. Of his second design (14, page 54) he says: 'A smaller double House than this is hard to be imagined.' It is a two-storey, hip-roofed house with end-stacks. Both the elevation and the ground-plan are identical with that of an even smaller house built in Dalkey, Co. Dublin in 1936. Of his third design he says: 'There may be some who love to make a great Show of a small Matter: in which case, the extent of this Front and the narrow Span of the Roof may chance to recommend it.' The plan is, in fact, virtually that of Mantua (8-11, pages 120-21) less the projecting bows at the ends, though the elevation is quite different.

Number V is a small three-bay, hip-roofed house, two rooms thick, with a bold cornice and parapet. There are five windows in the rere elevation, but Payne specifies that the parapet should be omitted from the side-walls, 'lest Rain or Snow might lie too long and do a signal Injury to the Walls by making them damp and less durable. He knew what he was talking about better than some modern observers who have attributed the omission of side-wall parapets to meanness, penury or ignorance.

Number VI is an L-plan house with a simple but pretty 'Palladian' frontispiece and a single great stack serving both arms of the L. One very interesting difference between the drawing in the manuscript and that published four years later is that the engraved version has a semi-circular bow at the back, absent in the original. This helps us to date the increasing popularity of bows, otherwise inadequately documented.

In his eighth design[57] he places two-bay, hip-roofed, single-storey wings abutting on to both ends of the main block, rather as at Kilcarty and Galtrim (1, page 164; 39, page 186) 'for it is impossible to have a Kitchen within a small House, without being annoyed at certain Times by offensive Smells arising from thence ... but this Mischief is quite prevented by putting the Kitchen out of Doors ... and for Regularity a good Room is added to the other end, and makes the left Wing; so that the Whole hath the Appearance of something grand .... The Porch taken off the Length of the Hall is not one of the least Conveniences in a Country-house.' This last-mentioned device, that of hollowing a porch out of the front and robbing it from the inner hall, is found in numerous houses in the Midlands, especially in Laois and Offaly, though most seem later than Payne's time, and this expedient, which is very well adapted to the Irish climate, was much favoured by Sir Richard Morrison half a century later.

No. IX (15, page 56) is a U-shaped house, with massive gabled projections at the back, giving a four-stack silhouette as at Creevaghmore (50, page 142). Here, as at Creevaghmore, the two rere wings are joined by a lean-to passage at ground level. The staircase, as at Creevaghmore, is in the front hall. Creevaghmore must be earlier than Payne's time, and I do not suggest that he necessarily knew it: rather that this type of house, gable-ended and with projecting wings containing kitchens, still-rooms and the like, facing the farmyard, was probably quite well-known and widely diffused.

In the tenth design he takes up a quarter of a block only 47 feet by 40 to accommodate a generous open-well staircase, and (in contravention of one of his own principles) has a secondary staircase behind the entrance-hall. To compensate, the kitchen is in a wing, 'But if such a mimic Grandeur should be disapproved of, the Kitchen must be made under the House.' No. XI (16, page 58) is a nearly square double-pile with a spine-wall and a pretty 'Palladian' doorcase, and 'The Back-front of the House may be finished with a Pediment.'

The twelfth and last design is somewhat archaic, being an H-plan house with a central hall. 'If it be thought to be an absurdity to have the best Room

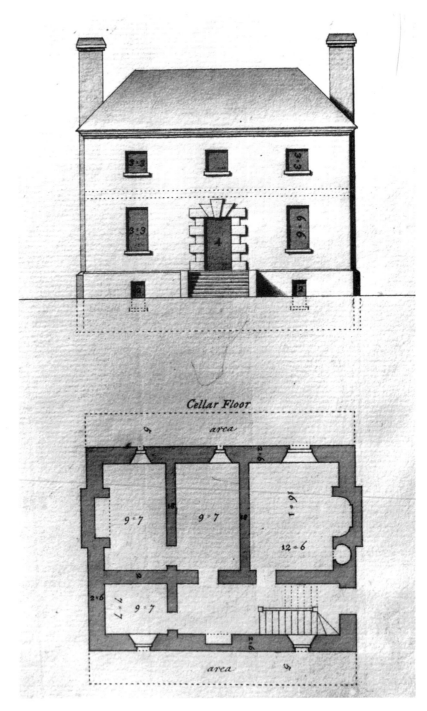

14 Plate 11 from the Reverend John Payne's *Twelve Designs for Country Houses*, published in Dublin in 1757, showing an elevation and plans for a small 'double house'.

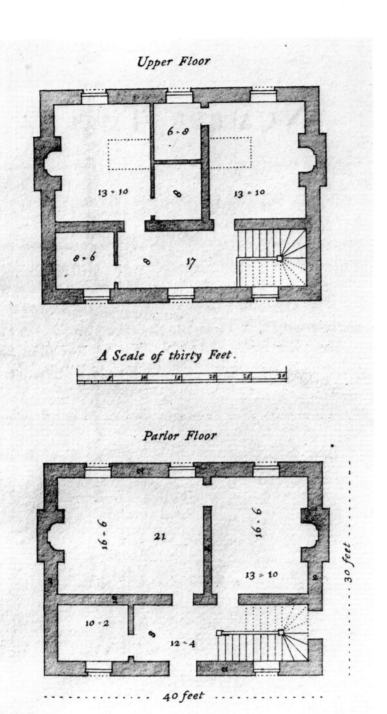

Upper Floor

6 × 8

13 × 10   8   13 × 10

8 × 6   8   17

A Scale of thirty Feet.

Parlor Floor

16 × 9   21   16 × 9

13 × 10

10 × 2

12 × 4

30 feet

40 feet

Num. IX

Ground Plan

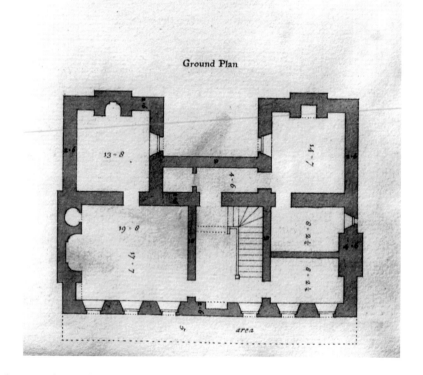

15 Plate IX from the Reverend John Payne's *Twelve Designs for Country Houses*, showing an elevation and plans for a U-shaped house with a four-stack silhouette.

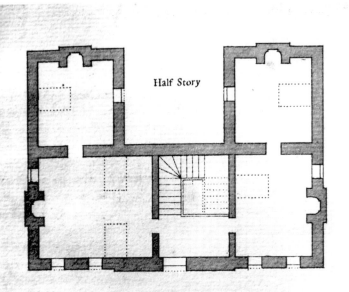

Half Story

A Scale of 30 Feet.

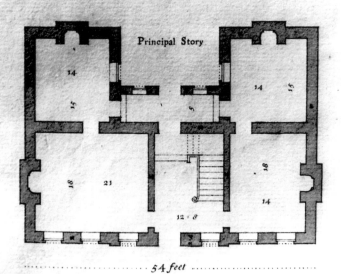

Principal Story

54 feet

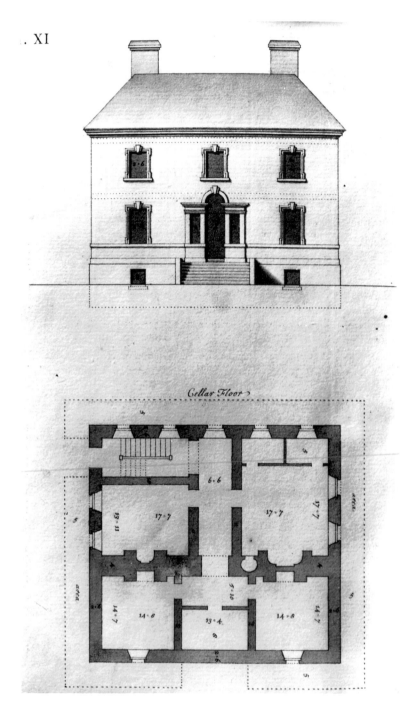

. XI

Cellar Floor

16 Plate XI from the Reverend John Payne's *Twelve Designs for Country Houses*, showing an elevation and plans for a nearly square double-pile with a spine wall.

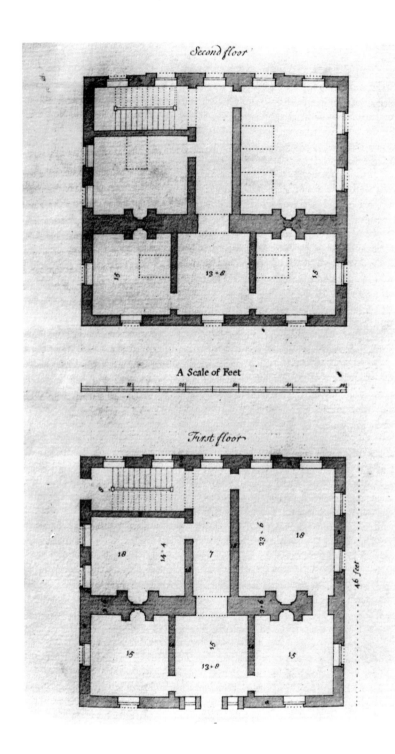

Second floor

A Scale of Feet

First floor

in the Place of a Hall, let it be remembered that both formerly and at this Day, the Hall, when it is large enough, was and is the chief Place of Entertainment; and surely on particular Occasions it may serve the same Purpose here, tho' there is no real, but only a seeming Grandeur intended.' I know of no house built during Payne's time which followed this model, but Vanbrugh had built himself just such a house, at Esher.

There are two interesting differences between the manuscript and the published book. In a number of cases, notably Nos 10 and 11, the elevations are less richly treated than in the manuscript: architraves, pediments to windows omitted, as though he did not wish to frighten off prospective builders by a show of expense. The other marked difference is that in the printed version the pitch of the main pediments has been lowered: in 1753 he draws them with a pitch approaching that of Athgoe, while in 1757 they approximate to his recommended proportion of a rise one-quarter of the width. It is as though his preference for the practicality of steep pitches were at war with the idea of correctness. We know, of course, that 'gable-pediments' of the Athgoe type were tending to die out in favour of more classical proportions.

On the subject of corner-fireplaces, he observes that 'angle-chimnies are at present much out of vogue' but he uses them nonetheless because of their obvious convenience in small house design. (In fact they were to last until Gandon's time, see 35, page 183.) As for dormers, 'Dormant Windows are now generally exploded.' It is true that they are rare in Irish building of the second half of the 18th century; but it is not always possible to be sure whether they were omitted in the first instance, or removed (as those at Durrow recently were) because of their vulnerability to the weather. Payne recommends lighting attics by small windows in the 'gable-ends'; and this is an observably common expedient even in the 17th century.

Finally, and a little surprisingly, he remarks in the manuscript (but not in the printed version) that wooden shingles are a common roof-covering. I do not know how much importance to attach to this, or to the fact that Payne omitted it in the printed version four years later. It is known that Castle Durrow of 1732 was originally roofed with shingles, and that they were used in the previous century.[58]

The list of subscribers to John Payne's book is interesting. It includes Francis Bindon (died 1765), Daniel Augustus Beaufort (1700–88), Nathaniel Clements (1705–77), all of whom were gentlemen-architects. Henry Darley and John Ensor and perhaps Robert Wills represent the trade or profession. John Wilde may possibly have been a builder. One would like to know why 'Master William Smyth' is down for a copy. The names of Pentland, Roberts, Mack and Semple are absent, but Arthur Jones Nevill, the recently deposed Surveyor-General, is there.

Another, nearly contemporary, book is of much less interest, though by a professed architect. This is John Aheron's *General Treatise of Architecture*, folio, Dublin 1754. Though a large and ambitious book, it has very little about smaller country houses in the section called 'Parsonages and Farmhouses from 100l to 500l expense'. Neither as a designer nor as a draughtsman is he to be compared with Payne: his plans are inconvenient and clumsily handled, and his elevations oscillate between dullness and pretension. As for the unpublished book of country house designs by Michael Wills (manuscript in the RIBA library, dated 1745), it is, if possible, even duller and more pretentious.

Much later in the century comes the folio of Sir Richard Morrison, *Useful and Ornamental Designs in Architecture*, Dublin 1793. This contains only five designs, and it is noteworthy that two out of the five are gable-ended, though even the smallest of them has elegant little wings. Morrison (1767–1849) went on to have a distinguished career in the following century. Needless to say, the standard English pattern-books circulated in Ireland, whether in the original English editions or in Dublin reprints, such as the 1768 James Williams reprint of Batty and Thomas Langley's *The Builder's Jewel*.

NOMENCLATURE

THE NOMENCLATURE OF IRISH HOUSES is a subject on its own. A large – perhaps the largest – number are called by a more or less anglicised version of the Irish name of the townland in which they stand. Of these, it need only be said that some of those who are conversant with the original find the corruption of the name at best irritating, at worst offensive; strangers are apt to find them baffling and are in constant difficulty over where to put the stress-accent; while to those who have been familiar with them since childhood, they are a constant source of pleasure. A similar number have names which are translations into Hiberno-English of the name in Irish: of such are the numerous names ending in '-town', specially prevalent in Meath and Kildare but found everywhere.

From the rest, the names are apt to have a distinctive flavour. Not always: for each Mount Equity or Fort Etna there are a dozen Beechwoods, Hollybrooks, Mount Pleasants and Bellevues variously spelt. Longfield and Roundwood do not exactly stretch the imagination. The enjoyment, or at least the hope, of connubial felicity is enshrined in countless names such as Lettybrook, Annsgift, Betty Ville or Palace Anne, and, with perhaps more poetic resonance, in Hymenstown, Bridestream and Rosegarland. A similar though less specific aspiration underlies such names as Summer Grove, Silverspring, Echo Hall and Harmony Hall. Elysium, Paradise and Heavenstown are eloquent: but so are Jockey Hall, Dog Hill, Whiskey Hall, Bachelors Lodge and Snugborough. Attachment to the reigning dynasty is touchingly expressed by Whigsborough and Mount Hanover. It is reassuring to know that even in the 18th century there was 'bad taste', bold and unashamed, as witness the existence, only a few yards apart, of Tallyho Lodge and Beau Peep Lodge on the borders of Galway and Roscommon. There is a pleasant line in Italianate names such as Piedmont, Mantua and Verona and perhaps Tourin (though this is probably just the 'little tower').

Few Irish houses have names of such stupefying banality as Claypotts, Floors, Maisons, Champs or Place: but there is a vein of heroic absurdity, however accidental its origin and however anachronistic our enjoyment, in Mount Hovel, Ballyruin, Ballyseedy, Ballydrain, Castle Dodard, Bumbo Hall, Ballynahaha, Tankardstown, Turbotstown and Castle Fish. Mount Bottom is, alas, only a misprint in the index of Phillips's *County Atlas of Ireland*. One would like to know – or perhaps it is better not to know – how Velvetstown and Mount Panther came by their names.

The flavour of these names evokes, to the adept, the flavour of the places themselves: long drives, often none too well maintained, through tussocky grasslands dotted with grazing cattle, over a rise or round a copse to the glimmer of pale limewash through dark foliage, till the house comes into view, with its door as likely as not standing open, facing the gravelled sweep, grass (more likely than not) growing out of the gutters, and, as *obbligato*, the distant clatter of the combine-harvester, the barking of the yard-dogs, or, most characteristic of all, the ubiquitous, clamorous cawing of the rooks.

PART II

THE BUILDINGS
ILLUSTRATED

I

1–2 G R A N E Y , *Castledermot, Co. Kildare*. In this early 17th-century house the close spacing of the windows away from the corners is very conspicuous. The stack on the right is unusual in being placed on the haunch of the gable instead of its apex. Behind and beyond it can just be seen the corner of the back wing.

The staircase was in the north wing and the principal rooms on the first floor, at which level there is a corbelled-out corner fireplace in the north-east corner of the main block. *Plan after William Garnerman*

THE EARLY
17TH CENTURY

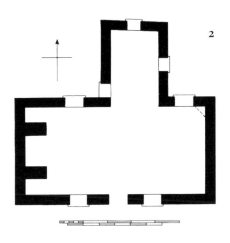

3   F E N N O R , *Slane, Co. Meath.* An example of
an early 17th-century end-stack house
incorporating a mediaeval tower-house, used as
the north limb of the 'T' and no doubt
containing the stair. The level marked 'l' is the
basement, and the ground slopes downwards
to the north. *Plan by D. Newman Johnson.*

15-16ᵗʰ century
17ᵃ century
more recent

4   B R A Z E E L   H O U S E ,
Knocksedan, Co. Dublin. Though
built in the 1630s and only eight
miles from Dublin, this house,
which was built for a Lord
Chancellor of Ireland, has a very
primitive plan. The stairs may have
been on the left just inside the
door. See page 10.
Plan after H. G. Leask

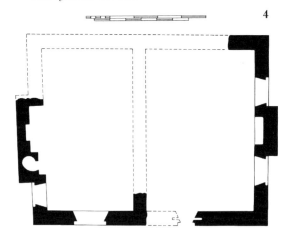

5

5-6 B R A Z E E L H O U S E Seen here from the south-west, the spacing and levels of the surviving windows at Brazeel raise many questions. The contrasted plaster finishes which have proved very resistant to the Irish climate are described by H. G. Leask in page 8 of this book. The surviving southern stack, shown in plate 6, with its arcading and decorative plaster pendants, cannot now be paralleled anywhere else in Ireland.

6

7

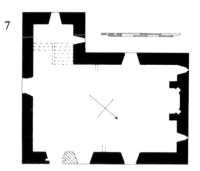

7 C A S T L E B A L D W I N , *Ballinafad, Co. Sligo.* An early 17th-century semi-fortified house (it has a machicoulis over the door) with the staircase in a projection at the rere. There is a reconstruction-drawing by H. G. Leask in Edward MacLysaght's *Irish Life in the Seventeenth Century.* The loops on each side of the ground-floor fireplace are at basement-level. *Plan after D. Waterman*

THE LATER
17TH CENTURY

I

I-3 LOWBERRY, *Ballinlough, Co. Roscommon.* The ruins of a small gable-ended house with a two-storey porch facing east, which appears to have had classical features. Ruined and of unknown date, this house more probably belongs to the 17th century than to the 18th. The plan, conjectural where shown dotted, much resembles that of Buncrana Castle, Co. Donegal (see 7, page 79) which is larger and probably later. The north-west room with its slopstone was no doubt the kitchen. The pistol-loops recall those at nearby Glinsk (which is earlier) and at Kiltullagh, Co. Galway (no doubt later: see 24-25, page 88). The front doorcase has the remains of a pediment, and the window over it is round-headed.

2

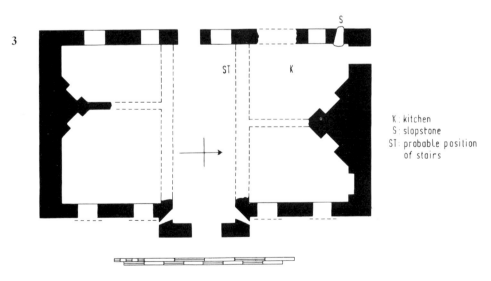

3

K: kitchen
S: slopstone
ST: probable position
   of stairs

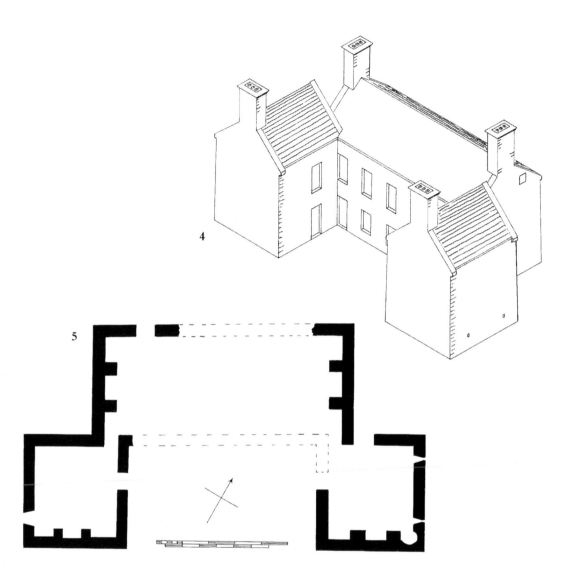

4-5   GORT, *Lecarrow, Co. Roscommon.* Certainly of the 17th century, and perhaps of its second half, this plan and isometric reconstruction show very curious relationship of the wings to the centre. Even odder is the jamming of openings right up against a re-entrant corner (for which the physical evidence is quite clear). The passages from the centre to the wings are only 2 feet 10 inches wide, in stone, so cannot have contained timber frames. The forward-facing gables without any openings in them are almost exactly paralleled at the much larger strong-house at Dromahair, Co. Leitrim. Gort itself is a twin of the house (similarly ruined) at Athleague, nine miles to the west and certainly by the same builders. According to Ordnance Survey evidence, Gort was evidently still occupied in 1838. The only conjectural element in this reconstruction is the fenestration of the centre block.

6

6 GORESGROVE, *Urlingford, Co. Kilkenny*. An instance of a house being added to, rather than superseding a tower-house. The massive stack with diagonal shafts suggests a date in the 17th century. There is a (now exposed) bond-timber extending over the door and three windows, so that it is a wonder that the front wall is still standing. If it were not a ruin it would probably have fallen down by now.

THE EARLY 18TH CENTURY

1700–1740

I

I SHANNONGROVE, *Pallaskenry, Co. Limerick.* The south (entrance) elevation and north elevation of one of the earliest houses of its (now rather
rare) type to survive in Ireland. The front door is dated 1709 and the back,
rather grander, 1723, a considerable interval. It is not very large, only 52
feet 6 inches by 42 feet, appreciably smaller all round than Roundwood,
Co. Laois: it is in fact almost exactly the same size as Kilduff, Co. Offaly.
Yet it gives the impression of being larger than either, partly owing to the
steps up to the doors, but mostly owing to the lofty steep-pitched roof and
the massive stacks which are unique in Ireland.

  The house was built for the Bury family, and though a John O'Brien
is mentioned as mason, there is reason to suspect the involvement of one
of the Rothery family as designer, especially since the building-owner's
monument of 1722 in the nearby church of Adare is signed 'Rothery fecit'
and has a cartouche of arms very similar to that over the north door of the
house. One of the Rotherys designed Mount Ievers only eight miles away
by crow, and Riddlestown, Co. Limerick, ten miles away in the opposite
direction, is probably also a Rothery house (see 53, page 108).

  Shannongrove is built of rubble stone rendered, but the two great
stacks are of brick: most unusual in being ribbed on plan and in having

English-style diaper-work in the brickwork. The stacks sit on a massive spine-wall, but the north-south divisions are by thin timber partitioning, much more usual in English practice than in Irish, where internal dividing-walls are usually robustly constructed, at least in the 18th century. This lends colour to the belief that the Rotherys may have been relatively recent immigrants from England, probably through Dublin where a William Rothery, mason, is found in the 1680s.[59]

The interior is almost completely panelled in the early style of wainscot, and the staircase has alternating fluted and twisted balusters and a pierced frieze, and a ramped rail. The arrangement of the recess in the south-west room on the ground-floor has been restored in the drawing (see 4, page 77) as seems probable from the physical evidence.

The drawings are based on the magnificent sixteen-sheet survey by Mr Howard Konikoff which he and Mr John Griffith have kindly allowed me to use. It is noticeable that on both fronts the basement windows have thick timber mullions and small panes. On the entrance front there is some similarity to Riddlestown, but on the north (river) front the basement windows are actually larger than those of the floors above, which is very unusual indeed. Another difference between the two fronts is that in the entrance-front the windows are grouped together towards the centre, leaving very wide solid corners as at Graney, Piedmont, Yeomanstown, Tober and Port Hall (again entrance-front, not river-front) while on the river-front they are much more widely spaced. It is difficult to imagine just what the house was like during the fourteen years between the date on the front door and that on the back one. Perhaps all that happened was that William Bury, inheriting the house in 1722 and marrying in 1723, commemorated both events by replacing a plain north doorcase with the present elaborate one carrying the arms of himself and his wife.

If, as has been suggested,[60] he also added the wings in that year, this is surprising, for they are very archaically furnished with large mullion-and-transom windows, just like those in the basement of the north elevation. The plan of the wings, and their relationship to the house, is very reminiscent of Lismore, Co. Cavan (23, page 88), and the resemblance may have been even closer if, as seems possible, Lismore had originally curvilinear gables facing forward, as at Shannongrove. It should be remarked that Mr Konikoff has restored these gables in the drawings: in real life they are almost gone, but some indications still remain.

The house has passed through many vicissitudes but happily still survives virtually intact and is being rehabilitated.

2   SHANNONGROVE
The north doorcase, on
which the carving is as
fine as that on any door-
case in Ireland, showing
the arms of Bury
impaling those of Moore.

3   SHANNONGROVE
Site-plan and north elevation of the house and
wings in which the
general resemblance of
the wings to those at
Lismore, Co. Cavan (23,
page 88) and a resem-
blance of a different kind
to those of Springhill, Co.
Derry (88, page 160) will
be clear.

2

3

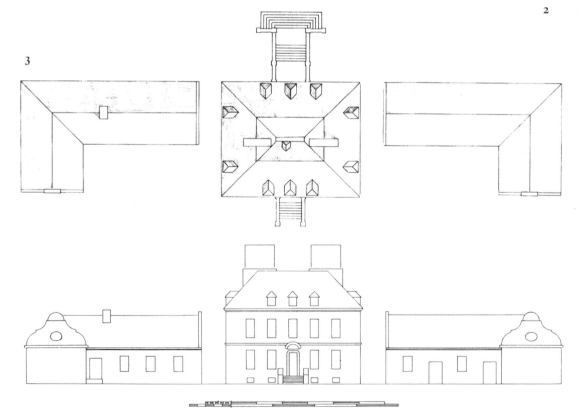

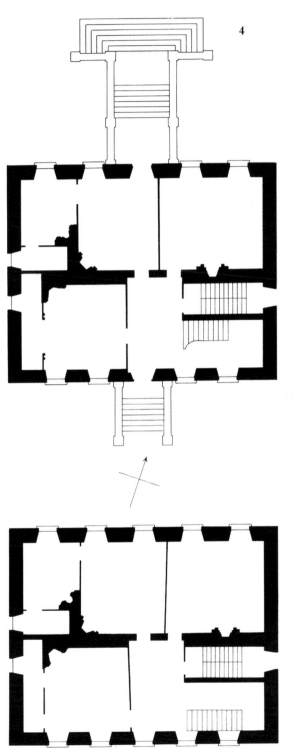

4   SHANNONGROVE In contrast to most other 18th-century houses shown in this book, an extreme thinness of the partitions (of timber) may be noted in these ground and first-floor plans, as also their slight obliquity.

5

5   KILMACURRAGH, otherwise WESTASTON, *Rathdrum, Co. Wicklow.* Documentary evidence in the possession of Mr Charles Acton dates this house to the first
decade of the 18th century. The wings were added in 1847–48. Its cornice and doorcase are of timber, which must once have been a common practice (as witness the
drawings of Francis Place done in the last years of the 17th century), but, apart from
a few examples such as the Red House, Youghal, Co. Cork, Molyneux House, Dublin
(demolished in the 1940s) and Eyrecourt (now rapidly falling down, as indeed is
Kilmacurragh), few survived into the 20th century in our climate. That of Woodlands,
Co. Dublin (28-29, pages 90-91) has doubtless been renewed. The roof structure of
Kilmacurragh is massive and apparently original.

6

6 BUNCRANA CASTLE,
Co. Donegal. Somewhat more
elaborate than its neighbour Linsfort
Castle (9, page 80), this house is four
years earlier, built by Henry Vaughan
in 1716. The interior is largely
panelled. The house is approached by
an axial bridge and a forecourt with
two hemicycles.

7 BUNCRANA CASTLE
In plan this building is an early
example of the house with
overlapping wings, as at Waringstown,
Co. Down and Lismore, Co. Cavan
(23, page 88). The two rooms to the
south-west are additions. Note the
corner fireplaces which are arranged
exactly as at Lowberry, Co.
Roscommon (1-3 pages 68–69).
Drawn by William Garnerman

8 BUNCRANA CASTLE
Doorcase with a tablet commemo-
rating the landing of Wolfe Tone at
Lough Swilly in 1798. There is a
similar but even better doorcase at
Hall Craig, Co. Fermanagh.

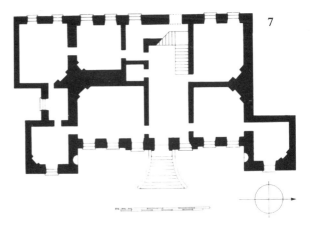

7

8

9

9 LINSFORT CASTLE, otherwise MOUNT PAUL, *Inishowen, Co. Donegal.* An H-plan house of 1720 with an armorial tablet recording its building by Captain Arthur Benson in that year.

10 CORBALLY, *Taghadoe, Co. Kildare.* An early 18th-century gable-ended house with a 'floating' pediment and four stacks. It represents, as does Kilcarty somewhat later, the middle ground between farmhouse and mansion: a shade unsophisticated but with great charm.

11 NEWCASTLE RECTORY, *Co. Dublin.* Built by Archdeacon Smyth in 1727, this house is typically Irish in its lack of a cornice. The square-headed doorcase with its segment-headed architrave is typically before *circa* 1740.

10

11

12

12 H A Y S T O W N , *Rush, Co. Dublin*. A brick house, only recently rendered, which has brick straight wings somewhat in the style of Vanbrugh, terminating in small pavilions which had steep pyramidal roofs. This doorcase, like that at Kilcrea only five miles away, is of the type found in Upper Castle Yard in Dublin, and, with the narrow windows with their flush frames, seems to suggest a date perhaps just in the first quarter of the 18th century.

13

14

13 KILCREA, *Donabate, Co. Dublin.* A small gable-ended house with a similar doorcase. Another such doorcase is found at Woodville, Harristown, Co. Kildare.

14 ALLENTON, *Tallaght, Co. Dublin.* This house was built early in the 18th century on to the front of an earlier house, forming, with it, a T. The earlier house stood till about twenty years ago but has now almost disappeared. The entrance-front, which faces north-west, was originally weather-hung.

15

15 BRIANSTOWN, *Cloondara, Co. Longford.*
Not, as it here appears to be, an early 18th-
century single-storey house, but a house
formerly of two storeys, reconstructed after a
fire in the present century. It was built in 1731
for Samuel Achmuty whose arms and motto
'Dum Spiro Spero' are in the tympanum. Above
this the two central windows had a niche
between them, and the house had a steep
hipped roof with three dormers. The
resemblance to Bonnetstown, Co. Kilkenny (31,
page 93) will be apparent.

16

16 CLONMANNON, *Rathnew, Co. Wicklow.*
A remarkable brick structure somewhat in the
style of Inigo Jones, it is not paralleled elsewhere
in Ireland, and is extremely difficult to date. It is
now among the outbuildings of a late 18th-
century house, but it seems once to have been a
house or part of a house in its own right.

17

17 FURNESS, *Naas, Co. Kildare*. A small ashlar-fronted house, probably of 1731, attributed to Francis Bindon (died 1765). Straight links (one here visible with a later added storey) tie the house to two-storey wings with cornices level with the platband of the main block, beyond which concave quadrants link these wings with kitchen and stable buildings. Clermont, Co. Wicklow, of 1730, has an almost identical elevation, but in brick with stone dressings. The staircase at Furness occupies a quarter of the plan, immediately to the left inside the front door.

18

18   GLOSTER, otherwise GLASTERRYMORE, *Shinrone, Co. Offaly*. Unusual in its length, its planning, and in many other ways, Gloster has features which can hardly derive from anyone other than Sir Edward Lovett Pearce (*circa* 1699-1733). Besides, the Lloyd family were his first cousins. This external west elevation, however, for all its charm, is provincial in almost every respect, and if Pearce was involved at all, he can hardly have been physically present.

19-20   GLOSTER The entrance-hall: the garden-front is behind the spectator and to his right. The date can hardly be later than 1730 and there is a strong flavour of Pearce about the concept, but would he have put that quarter-panel in the corner? In plate 20 showing the north wall of the entrance-hall, the garden-front is on the left. The very strong handling of the niches again suggests Pearce, but the execution is a little on the coarse side.

21-22   GLOSTER The upper hall, looking south-east. Two of the three openings into the entrance-hall are visible on the right, and in the middle is the south first-floor corridor. Plate 22 looks south across the upper hall, from the north corridor to the south corridor. Somebody has shaved off the top moulding of the 'dado, presumably because the archway was too narrow to get furniture through.

19   20

21

22

23

23 L I S M O R E, *Crossdoney, Co. Cavan.* This is necessarily a reconstruction elevation for although the long wings and one of the overlapping tower-wings still stand, the house is known otherwise only from old photographs of the front and back elevations. It was probably built before 1733, certainly well before 1739, and very possibly was designed by Sir Edward Lovett Pearce. The wings now have straight gables, but the inward-facing gables are curvilinear and the reconstruction suggested by the dotted lines seems possible.

24 K I L T U L L A G H, *Athenry, Co. Galway.* With gigantic panelled chimney-stacks and (as can still be traced) a very steep roof, this house, of two storeys over a basement, must have been very handsome. To judge by the provision of pistol-loops it was built early in the 18th century, or even earlier. The walls and stacks still stand to their full height. *Plan by William Garnerman*

25 K I L T U L L A G H In this elevation the roofline has been restored from indications given by the creasing on the stacks. Even in its present state it can be seen to be a building of quality. The pistol-loops commanding the entrance are conspicuous. *Elevation by William Garnerman*

25

24

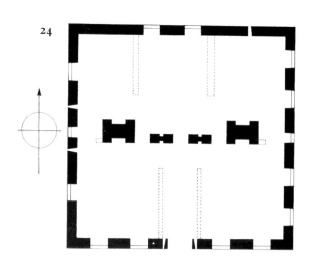

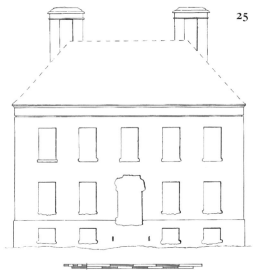

26

26 BOGAY, *Newtowncunningham, Co. Donegal*. The combination of end-stacks and hip-
roofs in this house is unusual but widespread. The stacks have typical diminution by
offsets. Like its fellow Oakfield, near Raphoe, it dates from the 1730s.

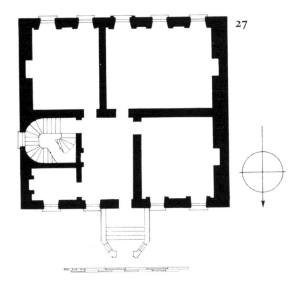

27

27 BOGAY It will be noted in
this plan that all the stacks are
in the outer walls. The porch is
later, but re-uses the original
doorcase.
Plan by William Garnerman

28

28-29 W O O D L A N D S , formerly C L I N S H O G H , *Santry, Co. Dublin*. Seen here from the east, Woodlands, or Clinshogh (Clonshagh) to give it the name by which it was known in the 18th century, is known to have been built before 1735, by the Reverend John Jackson, Vicar of Santry, from which village it lies a mile and a half to the north east. John Jackson and his brother Dan were both highly esteemed by Jonathan Swift, who in that year wrote to the Duke of Dorset: 'Mr Jackson … hath built a family-house, more expensive than he intended.' Exactly how expensive we do not know, but Elrington Ball[61] reports that tradition says it cost £800, and that it was locally known as 'Swift's House'. There are the usual myths about Swift or Jackson having designed it.

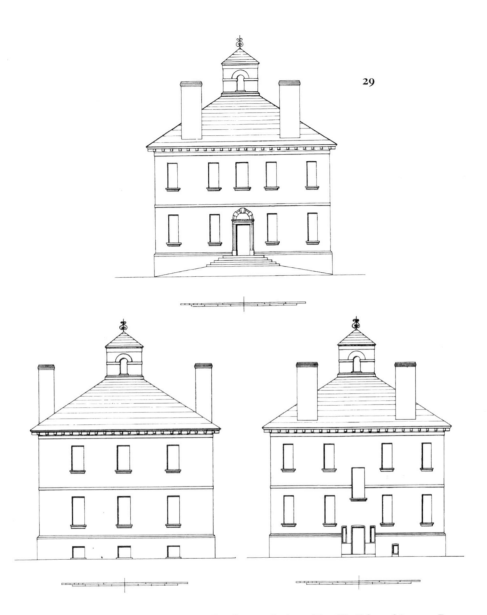

29

I have little doubt that Woodlands was designed by Sir Edward Lovett Pearce. The elevation of the entrance-front is a thinly disguised and most adroit adaptation of one of the end-elevations of Coleshill by Sir Roger Pratt, even to the part played by the chimney-stacks, and by the brick gazebo or lantern, corresponding in some sort to the timber one on the Coleshill roof. All four elevations are presentable and regular. The whole house is built in brickwork of admirable quality: the timber cornice, though convincing enough, must surely have been renewed. Only the front doorcase, which is obviously of the late 18th century, is a little discordant. In his drawing, John O'Connell has substituted a doorcase of a more likely type (see 29, above).

Woodlands is perhaps the most interesting small house of the early 18th century in the whole of Ireland. It is very small: only 42 feet square, and within this compass the elements of the plan are simply and logically disposed. The south-east room on the ground floor has an elegant Rococo ceiling decorated about the middle of the century. Though still privately occupied, it is menaced by the tide of the north Dublin suburbs, beginning to lap at its gates.

John Jackson's father and grandfather before him had been Vicars of Santry, and he himself had held the living since 1705. By the time that he built the house, presumably in about 1730, his four children were grown up. Swift seems to indicate that Jackson made journeys to London in 1728 and 1732 'upon some business': it is certain that he will have known Pearce. As far as we know, the whole of Pearce's architectural career in Ireland took place between 1726 and 1733. By 1731 he was well-known in London (as we know from Mrs Delany) to be an accomplished house-designer.

Swift, who had long exerted himself in vain to procure a deanery for Jackson, left him, in his will, his horses and mares, his horse-furniture, and his third-best beaver hat. In 1783, in the time of Taylor and Skinner, the house was called Clinshogh and was still inhabited by a Reverend Mr Jackson. Between then and 1837 its name was changed to Woodlands.
Drawings by John O'Connell

30

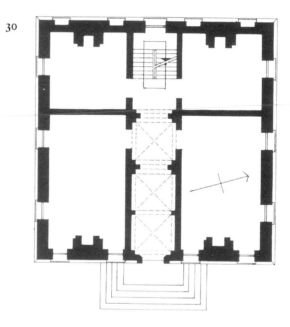

30   WOODLANDS The plan of this house is very Pearcean indeed. It is penetrated, from the front-door to the centre of the square, by Pearce's favourite device of a corridor of square compartments, in this case groin-vaulted. On the innermost of these stands the tower which ascends through the building to shoot finally out through the top of it. *Plan by John O'Connell*

31

31 B O N N E T S T O W N , *Co. Kilkenny*. One of the coign-stones in this house is dated 1737 and its fellow records the name of the owner, Samuel Matthews. The house is of tripartite plan, with the staircases at the back. The even number of windows is reproduced on the back elevation, but there are two large central windows at mezzanine level with a central door between and beneath them. The way in which the front door and flanking windows are tied together is reproduced in a simplified form at Brianstown, Co. Longford which is dated 1731: both resemble Sir Edward Lovett Pearce's design for Luke Gardiner's house in Henrietta Street, Dublin. The Bonnetstown roof is gracefully sprocketed. The plan of Castle Ffrench, Co. Galway (14-15, page 173) some forty years later is virtually identical.

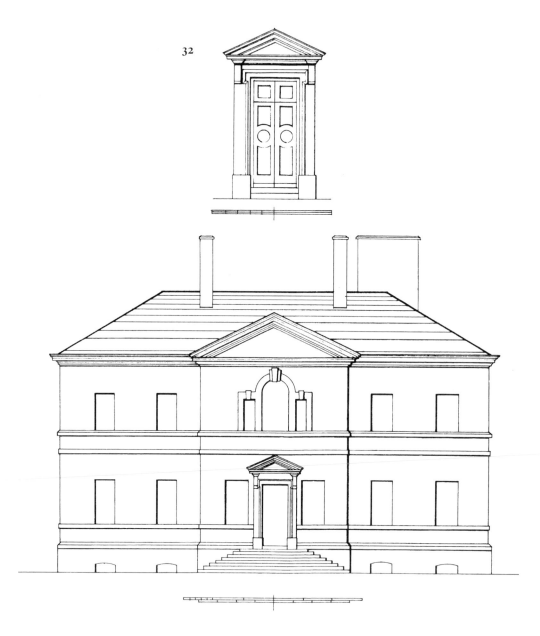

32 C U B A C O U R T , *Banagher, Co. Offaly*. Cuba Court is, or rather was, perhaps the most splendidly masculine house in the whole country. The south and west fronts shown here are treated with equal and considerable grandeur. Apart from its splendid proportions and tremendous scale, its most striking features are the massive cornice which crowns three sides and most of the fourth, and the west doorcase, of Michelangelesque deriva-tion but here taken, no doubt, from Vanbrugh's King's Weston (see 34, page 96). It was hip-roofed with the slopes draining directly to the great cornice, and the thickness of the walls is apparent even from photographs of it in a state of ruin (35-36, page 97).

The plan, which has been recovered by Jeremy Williams and John O'Connell, is ambiguous. The grander of the two pediments is to the west, and the more striking of the two doorcases. Yet this doorcase gave access latterly to a rather narrow passage, while the large central room in the south front looks like a hall. The south front with its quasi Venetian window, its pedestal course and the disposition of the chimneys, has echoes of Lismore, Co. Cavan (23, page 88). There was apparently provision for a circular staircase in the manner of the Queen's House, Greenwich, opening east off the south hall, but it seems not to have been built. At the back, in the depth of the recess, was a steep gable, as so often at the backs of houses where a gable would not have been tolerated at the front.

Cuba is without doubt the work of a learned architect. It is not far from Gloster – some fourteen miles – and the learning and the confidence of the design suggests the participation of Sir Edward Lovett Pearce. But documentary support is lacking. The house is said to have been built by a family called Fraser, but by the late 18th century it was in the hands of the Dalys. It became a school in the early 19th century, and for a moment in 1854 we glimpse it by the same light that was shed on one of the most famous schools in imaginative literature. 'It is very large and looks externally like a gentleman's country-seat – within most of the rooms are lofty and spacious, and some – the drawing-room, dining-room &c handsomely and commodiously furnished. The passages look desolate and bare – our bedroom, a great room of the ground floor, would have looked gloomy when we were shown into it but for the turf fire that was burning in the wide old chimney.' The writer was Charlotte Brontë, spending her honeymoon with the Reverend Mr Nicholls, who had been brought up in the house by his uncle Dr Allen Clarke Bell, the Master of the school. Cuba was unroofed some thirty years ago, and less than two complete walls of it now stand: one of the most lamentable of the casualties of peace.

Elevations by John O'Connell

33

33 CUBA COURT
The south front
photographed in
1957, since when
further demolition
has taken place.
Through the
tripartite window
on the first floor
can be seen the one
at the back, in the
narrow re-entrant
courtyard.

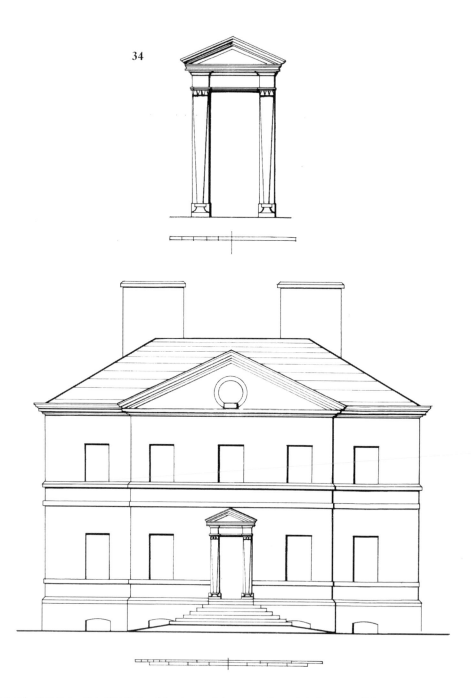

34

34-36 C U B A C O U R T In this view of the west front it is just possible to see how thick the walls are, and how several courses of slating can rest directly on the thickness of the wall plus the projection of the cornice. Plates 35 and 36 show the west doorway, based on Sir John Vanbrugh's King's Weston (1711-14).
Drawing by John O'Connell

35

36

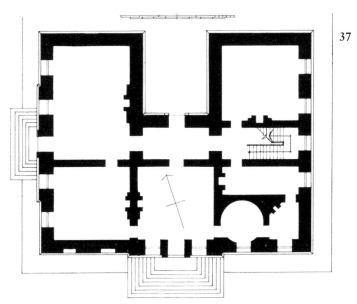

37

37 C U B A C O U R T In plan this building was a rectangle with a deep recess in the middle of the back which faces north. The (later) wall on the north side of the passage to the west door has been omitted. *Drawing by John O'Connell*

38

38 LEDWITHSTOWN, *Ballymahon, Co. Longford*. Though of exceptionally sound construction, Ledwithstown, photographed here in 1959, was in an advanced stage of dilapidation, from which it has been happily rescued by its owners. There can be few houses of its size in Ireland more thoroughly designed, and with internal decoration so well integrated. Though a little larger than Woodlands, Co. Dublin, it is still very small, only 48 feet by 47 feet overall: yet all the elements of the plan are very convincingly interrelated, and the attribution to Richard Castle (*circa* 1690–1751) seems reasonable, though without conclusive documentary support. There are in the collection at Castle Coole, Co. Fermanagh, some drawings for a small country house by Richard Castle which have some resemblance to Ledwithstown and help to support the idea that he was its architect. In the late 18th century the Reverend Mr Palmer lived in the house.

In spite of its small size, it is provided with two staircases, opposite one another off the back end of the hall, in the manner of Cashel Palace. That to the left is the main staircase: the other is narrower and debouches at the side door in the basement (compare Kilduff, Co. Offaly). The hall is relatively large and has a decorative fireplace of Kilkenny black marble, like that in the north-west room on the first floor.

The larger rooms of the ground floor face north, but there are windows on all four fronts. The east and west fronts come out more or less regularly, but in the north front the spacing of the windows is for internal effect.

Many of the internal cornices are of plaster on brick cores, as at Cuba Court, and the panelling of the ground floor is mainly in plaster, with occasional decorative touches of baskets and shells. Upstairs it is, or was, of timber. In the basement the central three-bay corridor has pretty groin-vaulting in brick. A great deal of brick is used in the interior, though the external finish is rendering over rubble masonry, as at Eyrecourt.

There are no round-headed openings except staircase-windows, and the entrance-front relies entirely on coigns, architraves, the main cornice, and the pediment over the front door and sidelights. Two massive stacks, both wider than the distance between them, complete the composition. It stands in a lonely situation not far from Lough Ree in County Longford: its nearest neighbour the enigmatic Castle Cor. (89, page 161)

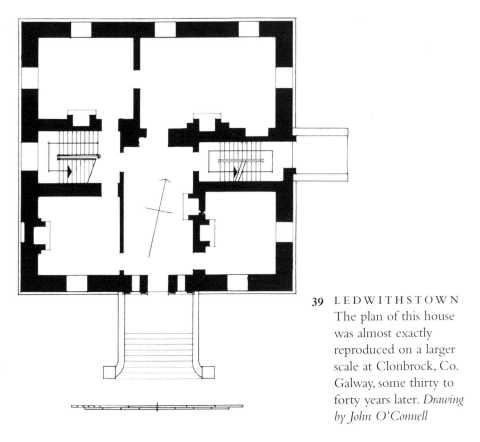

39

39 LEDWITHSTOWN
The plan of this house was almost exactly reproduced on a larger scale at Clonbrock, Co. Galway, some thirty to forty years later. *Drawing by John O'Connell*

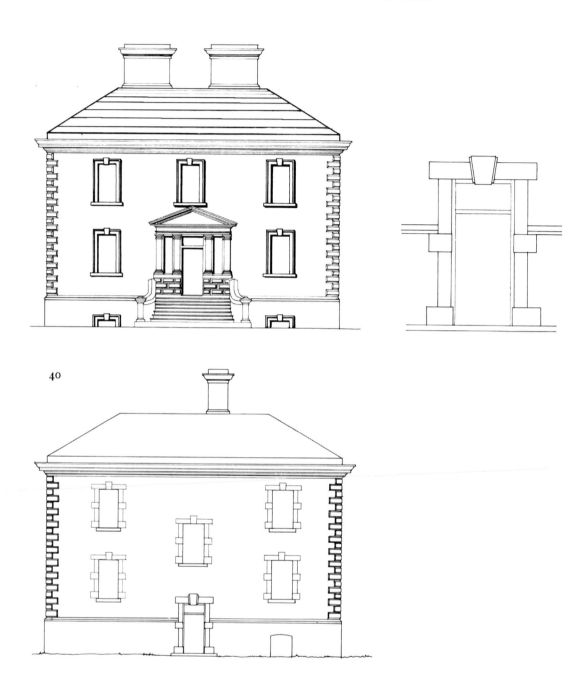

40

40 LEDWITHSTOWN The present parapet at Ledwithstown is of inferior materials and probably not original. In the south and east elevations given here, it has been omitted and the roof-cornice junction restored on the model of the Provost's House, Trinity College, Dublin and Leinster House, which seems as likely as anything. *Elevations by John O'Connell*

41

41 GAULSTOWN, *near Castlepollard, Co. Westmeath*. Not to be confused with the more famous Gaulstown further south in the same county, this enigmatic little house is of unknown but probably early 18th-century date. The back elevation has a rather steep gable and a tripartite opening on the principal floor similar to the door and sidelights on the front, but with no projection. It belonged in the 18th century to a family called Lill, who are found also at Stewartstown, Co. Tyrone and Dalkey, Co. Dublin. Like Ledwithstown, this house has now been restored.

42

42 MOUNTAINSTOWN, *Kells, Co. Meath*. This is a somewhat naive but charming building, its giant Ionic order lacking an architrave and frieze. The doorcase and steps, however, are well designed and accomplished in execution, both in carved stone and wrought iron.

43 GOLA, *Scotstown, Co. Monaghan*. This elevation, in which the scale is approximate only, has been reconstructed from engravings in E. P. Shirley's *History of Monaghan* and in Sir Bernard Burke's *Visitation of Seats and Arms*. This very striking house, which seems to have disappeared about fifty years ago, is provincial, no doubt, but has some interesting affinities. The segment-headed ground-floor windows suggest an early date, but the square lanterned attic seems to derive from Pearce's Woodlands. It appears to have been made of masonry or brick, and if so it must have stood on a suitable plan-structure. This, together with the Venetian window, suggests that it was a provincial derivative of the Pearce school. (It can be assumed that the wings are somewhat later than the main block.) Only eight miles away a surviving though much altered house, Anketell Grove, Emyvale, shows some relationship with Gola, though its central attic-tower now exists in 19th-century form. It has quadrants and wings with gothick windows, but the massing of the main block is very like that of Gola, and neither house much resembles any elsewhere, so that it is difficult not to assume some connection between them.

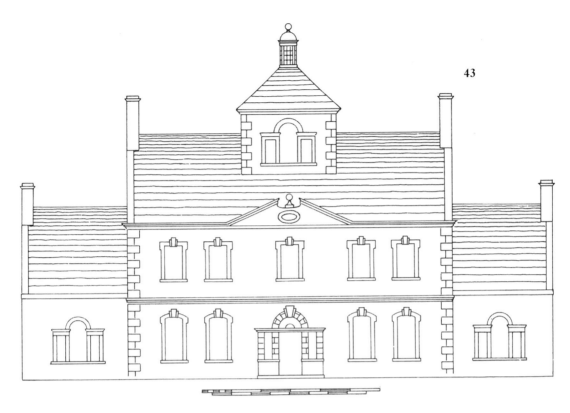

43

44

44 DUNSTOWN, *Kilcullen, Co. Kildare.* Similar to Sherwood Park (44-47 page 140), with less formality in most respects, though more in the provision of pediments to the wings. The baseless pediment-gable of this house has had barge-boards added to it in the last century, but the original doorcase has a touch of cut-stone formality.

45 GARRETTSTOWN, *Ballinspittle, Co. Cork.* Two blocks with identical elevations face one another across a forecourt: this photograph shows the service-block (still roofed) seen through the front door of the block which, with enlargements, became the house and is now ruinous. The house proper, which would have been out of the picture to the right, seems never to have been built.

46 DRUMCONDRA HOUSE, now ALL HALLOWS' COLLEGE, *Co. Dublin.* The south front of this building, shown here to the left, is by Sir Edward Lovett Pearce: the very enigmatic east front, to the right of the photograph, is presumably earlier and there is nothing much resembling it anywhere else in Ireland. The plan of this house is a botch, re-botched at least once.

46

45

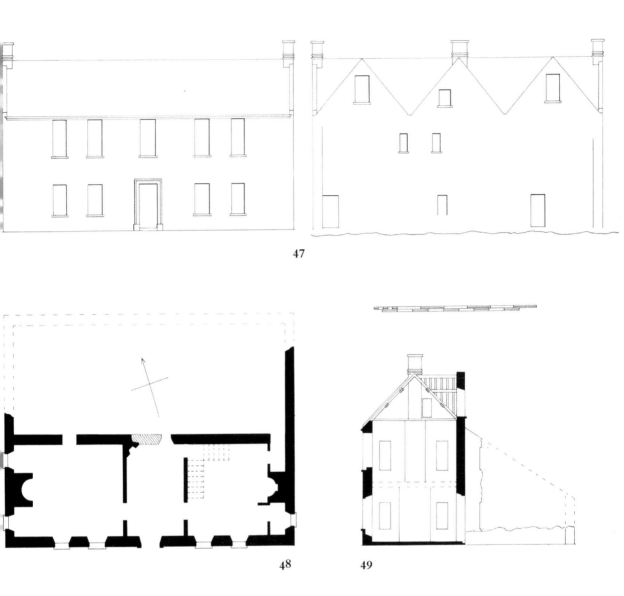

47

48   **49**

47-49 PIEDMONT, *Cooley Peninsula, Co. Louth.* The south (entrance) and north elevations, plan and section of this perplexing early 18th-century house (page 10) are
based on a survey by the Office of Public Works, Dublin. For a discussion of this
house, see page 10. The position of the inward-facing walls of the two lean-tos at
the back is conjectural, but fixed between obvious limits. In its last phase two of
the front windows on each floor (the second and fourth) had been blocked, and
the five remaining windows had been reduced in height, which particularly
improved the proportions of those on the first floor. The house is now derelict.

50

50 DOLLARDSTOWN, *Slane, Co. Meath*. This building was a remodelling in red brick, probably by Richard Castle, of an earlier house. Castle's favourite central niche and oculus, as seen at Rochfort, otherwise Tudenham, Co. Westmeath, and elsewhere, is visible above a doorcase with a noble Doric pediment and joinery taken from William Salmon's *Palladio Londiniensis: or The London Art of Building*. On the left of the photograph is one of Dollardstown's two tower-like wings. Round the corner in plate 51 there is a riot of Venetian windows.

51 DOLLARDSTOWN This north-west face of the house shows well-nigh every possible permutation of the Venetian window theme. Note especially the projecting blind tympanum in the first floor back, the very unusual glazing of the principal windows on the flanking wall, the reversal of the roles of brick and stone in the basement, and the panels in the parapet-attic.

51

52

52 TOBER, *Dunlavin, Co. Wicklow.* An early 18th-century house, its windows grouped closely together away from the corners, and irregularly spaced on the ground floor.

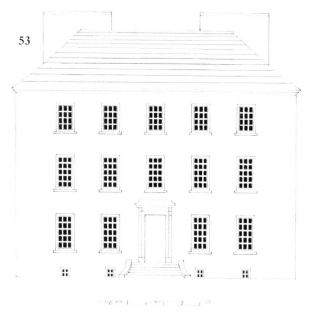

53

54

53 R I D D L E S T O W N , *Rathkeale, Co. Limerick*. Probably of about 1730–40, related both to Shannongrove and to Mount Ievers, this house was formerly panelled internally but lost its panelling many years ago. The glazing-bars have been restored in this elevation. The house is of rubble stone, rendered, only the door-case and cornice being of cut stone.

54 Y E O M A N S T O W N , *Curragh, Co. Kildare*. An early 18th-century house with curvilinear end-gables (doubtless rebuilt), a 'floating' pediment, and a very marked grouping of the windows away from the corners. It is built of brick, though now rendered, and is one of the very few Irish houses to have undulating arrises to the heads of its upper windows.

55

55 SEAFIELD, *Donabate, Co. Dublin.* A building of villa-plan, though gable-ended, this is one of the few houses of its size in Ireland to have a two-storey hall. Its tripartite plan owes obvious debts to Pearce's villa-designs, and even the portico seems to owe something to Pearce's portico at Bellamont Forest, though more coarsely executed, in granite. This is the south front: the staircase is in the far left-hand or north-west corner, and there is a flying gallery across the north end of the hall to provide communication between the east and west parts of the first floor. The space covered by the portico is partly inside and partly outside the line of the main front wall, as indicated by the settlement in way of the top windows. These top windows, with their very 'Italian' proportions, have a near-parallel in Grove House, Miltown, Co. Dublin, recently demolished.

The hall has a tolerably correct statement of superimposed Ionic and Corinthian pilasters, and several rooms have good panelling. Whether the house was new-built or, as seems less likely to me, a reconstruction within the old walls, the work was probably done after 1737.[62] The hall has good grisaille paintings.

56

56 SEAFIELD The three gables here on the north front correspond with the three small hip-roofs on the south front, and may be compared with the treatment at the rere of Piedmont, Co. Louth (47-49, page 105).

57 SEAFIELD The ground and first-floor plans of Seafield form a very complete and unaltered example of the tripartite Palladian villa-plan, but with Baroque overtones. The portico *in antis*, half in and half out of the rectangle, recalls Alessandro Galilei at Kimbolton or James Gibbs at Sudbrook, while the possession of a double-height central hall, and the giving of two windows to each flanking room (instead of one as in the typical Palladian villa) recalls Thomas Archer's Marlow Place. The whole conception is very close to Pearce's studies Nos 3, 67 and 74 in the Proby Collection. Communication between the two sides at bedroom level is by the bridge across the north end of the hall.

Only a slight awkwardness in the handling (for example the plan-form of the responds of the *antae*, and the uncertain spacing of the pilasters to the flanking-walls of the hall) discourages the attribution of the building to Pearce. It is, even so, certain that Seafield is a building of the Pearce school, and even possible that the design was outlined by him and executed by someone else.
Drawings by Derry O'Connell

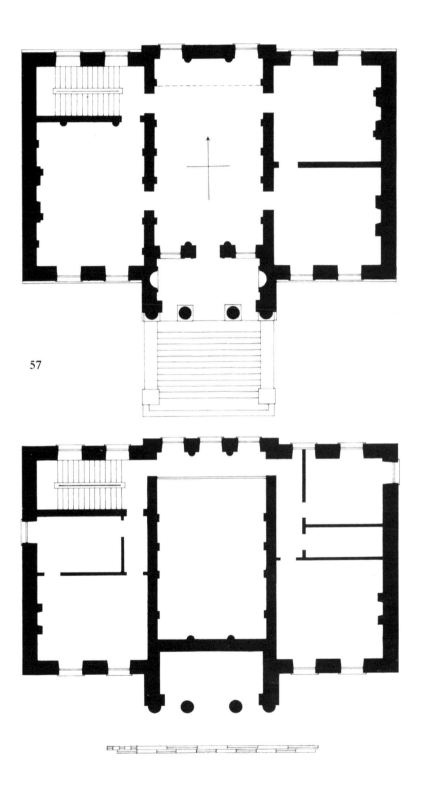

57

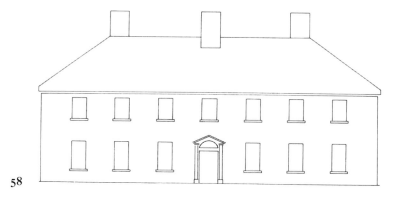

58

58 AGHABOE, *Ballybrophy, Co. Laois.* Of uncertain date, but probably dating to the first half of the 18th century, this house had formerly small wings with tripartite openings to right and left. That to the right (not shown on this drawing) survives after a fashion: that to the left has disappeared. Both have the appearance of being additions, being disproportionately small in relation to the main block, which may have received its mid-century doorcase at the same time.

59 DROMARD, otherwise MOUNT BROWN, *Rathkeale, Co. Limerick.* This building is a fine example of the plan-form seen also at Longfield. The end-bays are here only one-storey high, and the staircase behind the hall is rectangular, and the stacks set transversely instead of fore-and-aft; but the relationship is nevertheless clear. The entrance-hall has a Doric cornice with mutules, and the doorcases are eared, suggesting a date in the first half of the 18th century.

59

60

60 BALLYSALLAGH, *Johnswell, Co. Kilkenny*. Like some other early-to-mid 18th-century houses, Ballysallagh has a platband instead of a cornice, and the platband does duty for the bedmould of the pediment. The end-coigns are bolder and better-finished than those of the breakfront. The hall is narrow, as indicated by the stacks; and a full-height projection in the centre of the rere contains the staircase.

61   62

61-62 M O U N T H A N O V E R , *Duleek, Co. Meath.* Probably dating from the first half of the 18th century, this house has typically thick glazing-bars and fine ironwork (see page 43). The characteristic heads to the narrow sunken panels in the door-jambs are worth notice. In essentials, this house has a plan resembling that of Dysart, Co. Westmeath (see page 135). A view from the south-east, showing the disposition of gables and stacks, is given in plate 62.

63

63 U L L A R D ,
Graignamanagh, Co. Kilkenny. An extremely well-proportioned house of the first half of the 18th century, with a subtly sprocketed roof. The smooth-rendered strips at the corners of the building are an undesirable modern treatment sometimes applied also to churches, and thoroughly to be reprobated. The house faces the roofless Romanesque church of Ullard.

THE MID‑18TH CENTURY
1740‑1770

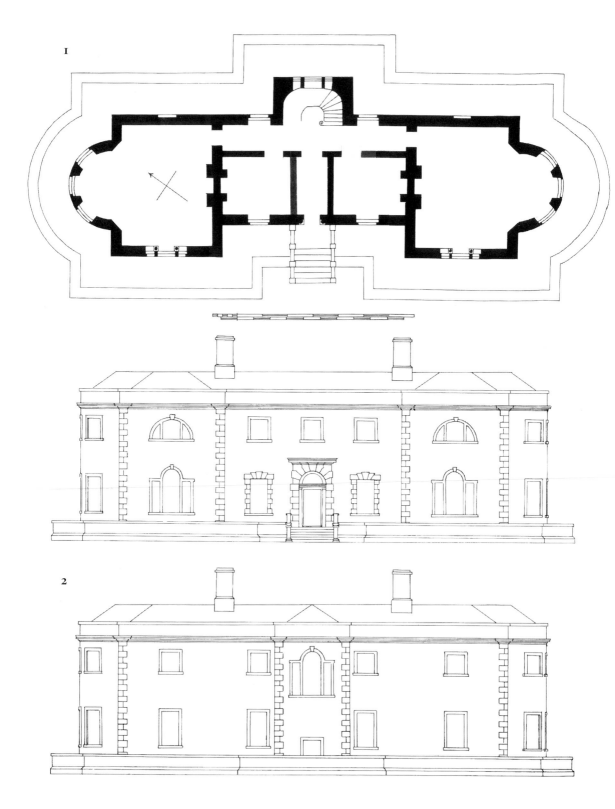

I

2

1–2 B E L V E D E R E , *Lough Ennell, Co. Westmeath.* Though nearly 100 feet long, Belvedere, with its strange elongated plan (later added to at the back) is not really a large house. Built in about 1740 for Robert Rochfort Lord Belfield and designed by Richard Castle, it may perhaps be the earliest bow-ended house in the country. In his drawings of the front and rere elevations, David Griffin has rectified later alterations, most conspicuously the unhappy alteration of the Diocletian windows in the 19th century, since rectified. He thinks that the front elevation may derive from the rere elevation of Pearce's Bellamont Forest, and he may well be right. The chamfered internal corners of the bow-ended rooms are a very surprising feature. A full description of the house is given in Desmond Guinness's and William Ryan's *Irish Houses and Castles.*

3-5 A N N E V I L L E , *Mullingar, Co. Westmeath.* Probably built in conjunction with Belvedere in the 1740s. The entire basement is elaborately vaulted. The central projection is polygonal outside and semi-circular inside. The basement and top floor windows retain their 2-inch glazing bars, with square blocks at the intersections. *Drawings by John O'Connell*

3

4

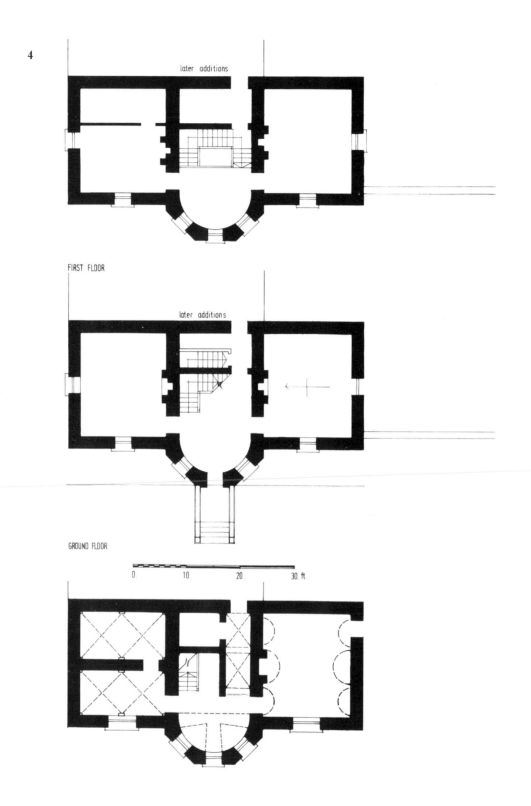

later additions

FIRST FLOOR

later additions

GROUND FLOOR

0   10   20   30 ft.

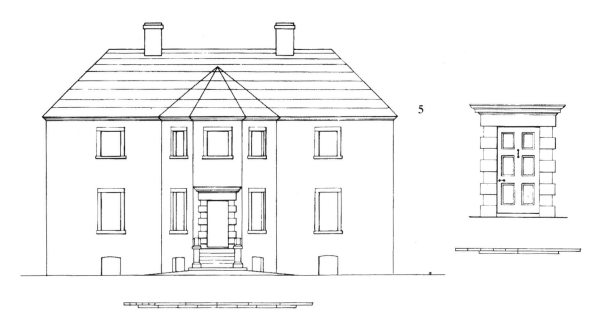

5

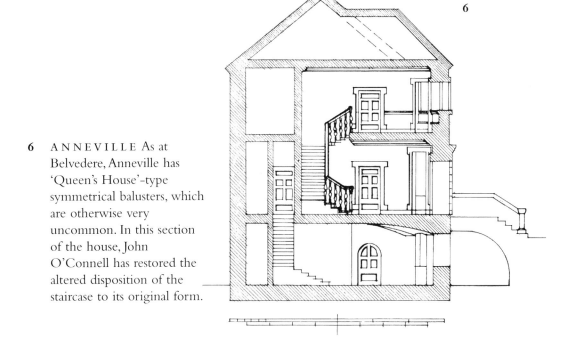

6

6 ANNEVILLE As at
Belvedere, Anneville has
'Queen's House'-type
symmetrical balusters, which
are otherwise very
uncommon. In this section
of the house, John
O'Connell has restored the
altered disposition of the
staircase to its original form.

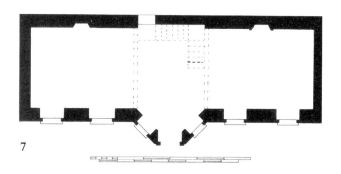

7

7 VIANSTOWN, *Downpatrick, Co. Down.* Though small and primitive in plan, this house had a fine fully classical doorcase, the setting of which, in a three-sided projection, recalls Ballyraheen, Co. Wicklow, and Mount Gordon, Milcum and Milford, all in County Mayo. Plan after the *Co. Down Archaeological Survey*

8

8 MANTUA, *Swords, Co. Dublin.* In this general view of Mantua (see also page 18) the porch is modern and made of concrete. The house has now been demolished.

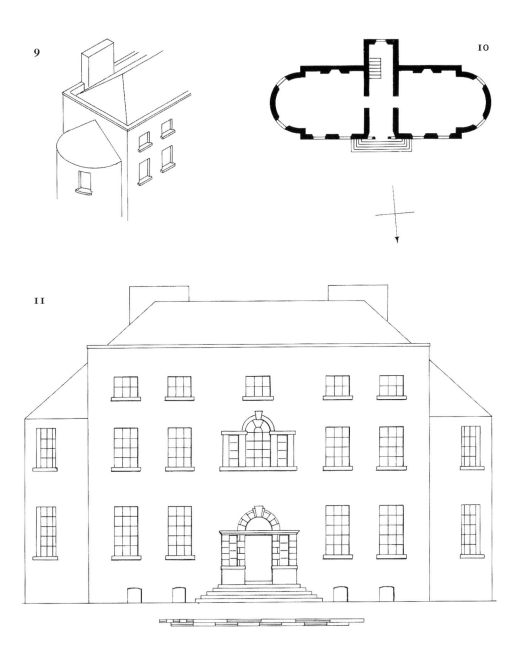

9-11 M A N T U A For some years before its final destruction, the modern porch shown in 8 obscured the doorcase. The doorcase illustrated here is largely conjecture but based on the recollections of David Griffin.

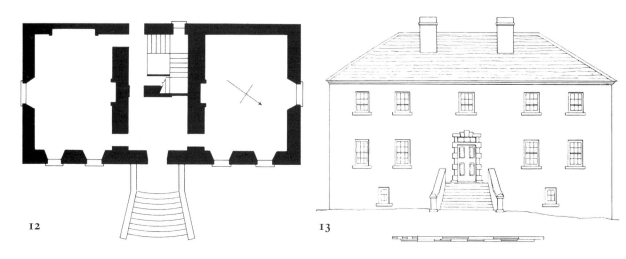

12

13

12-13 C A R R O W N A C O N , *Co. Mayo*. The basement of this mid 18th-century house is well above the ground and has its own window-spacing.
Elevation by William Garnerman

14

14 B A L L Y N A H O W N
C O U R T , *Co. Westmeath*.
This mid 18th-century
building is one of the rare
brick houses in the
Central Plain, though not
far from the Shannon at
Clonmacnoise. The
pediment over the door is
somewhat provincial.
Note the central stack.
The date of the building
is 1746, as attested by a
rainwater-head bearing
the initials of Edmond
Malone and his wife
Ruth.

15 PORT HALL, *Lifford, Co. Donegal.* This house was built by Michael Priestley in 1746 for John Vaughan of Buncrana Castle (6-8, page 79). The east front, towards the river Foyle, is plainer. Few Irish houses have an attic above the cornice, as here, but many have the kind of intermediate pediment-gable seen here, and repeated on the river-front, which has no break in the centre but is flanked by lower buildings at right-angles (just visible in this photograph) forming a deep court.

16 CASTLE BLUNDEN, *Co. Kilkenny.* A mid 18th-century house still lived in by the Blunden family. There are two gables carrying stacks at the back, and between them a wide and deep projection containing both the main and secondary staircases, and making the plan a T.

16

17

18

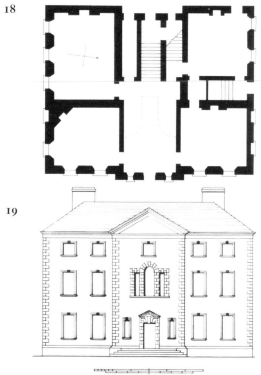

19

17–20 R O U N D W O O D , *Mountrath, Co. Laois.*
This house, the entrance front of which is
shown in plate 17, has several anomalous
features. The doorcase, for example, which
is of limestone, in contrast to the sand–
stone of the rest of the elevation, has a
somewhat larger vertical module than the
building as a whole (contrast for example
Sherwood Park in plate 47, page 140
which is the other way round). The
detailing of the Venetian window over it
is clumsy, and again the coursing differs
from that of the coigns. The moulded sills
and fluted keystones are somewhat
archaic for the presumed date of about
1750. It has been suggested that
Roundwood was designed by Francis
Bindon: I prefer to believe that it was just
put together by somebody: master–builder
or even owner.
Elevation and section by John O'Connell

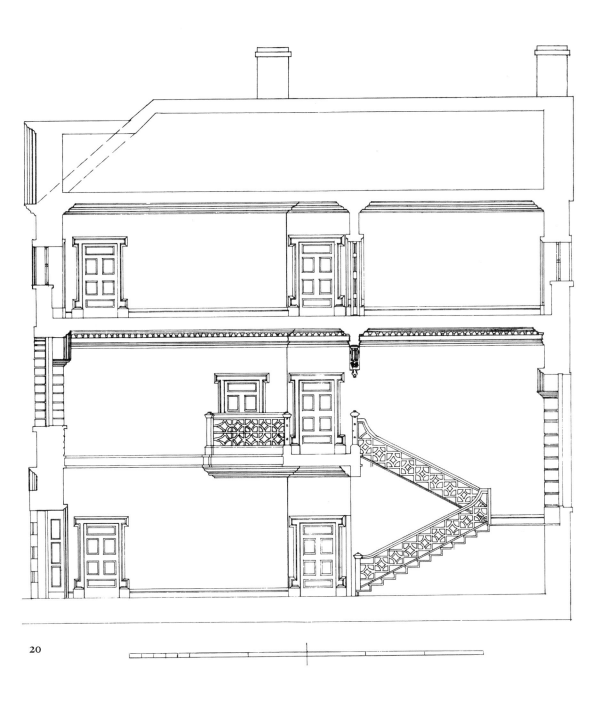

20

21 ROUNDWOOD The entrance hall and staircase: the gallery gives access to the bedrooms to right and left.

22

23

22-33 NEWHALL, *Ennis, Co. Clare*. A red-brick house attributed to Francis Bindon, of about 1750. The ground-floor windows have been widened and their sills lowered. It is uncertain whether the range at the back, making the whole into a T, is an earlier house or not: in its present form it is apparently of 19th-century date. The entrance-hall contains an elaborate organ case, but the case contains no organ. A detail of the doorcase at Newhall is given in plate 23.

24

24-25 COOPERHILL,
Co. Sligo. This house,
which was begun in
1755 and not finished
till 1774, has been
attributed to Francis
Bindon. Built of
locally quarried
ashlar, it has a fine
bold cornice, as have
nearly all Bindon's
houses. The doorcase
and inner hall
doorway are shown
in plate 25.

25

26-30 S U M M E R G R O V E, *Mountmellick, Co. Laois*. The exact date of Summer Grove is not known. A family of Huguenot origin called Sabatier were the builders. They acquired the lands in 1736, but it seems to me unlikely that the house could have been built very soon afterwards, as has been suggested. There was not much stylistic evolution between the death of Richard Castle in 1751 and that of Nathaniel Clements in 1777, especially in the provinces, where the influence of Ducart, for example, was stylistically conservative. The prominence given to the roof at Summer Grove makes it look like an earlier house – Cuba Court for example. Yet the house gives a strong impression that it is all of a piece: that the elevations, the plan and the internal decorations are contemporary; and the decorations can hardly be earlier than about 1755.

Apart from its obvious charm and its substantially unaltered state, the main interest of Summer Grove lies in the ingenuity of the planning. In the back half of the house three storeys are fitted into the same height as two on the entrance-

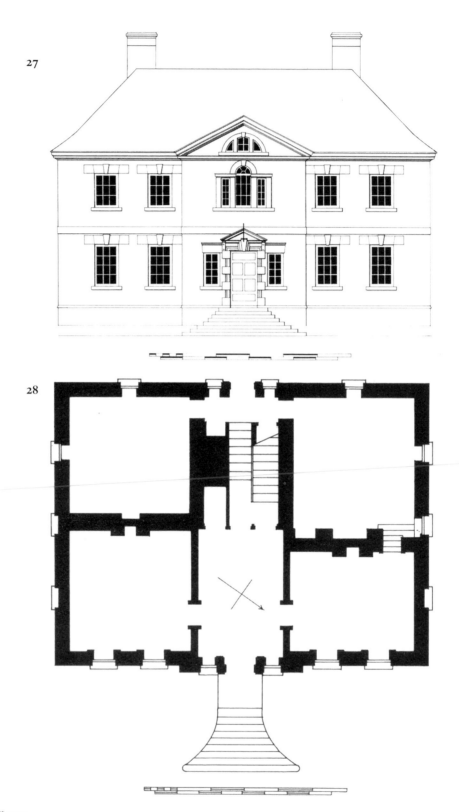

27

28

29

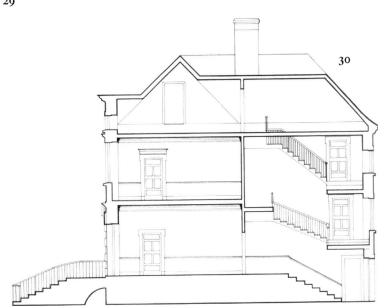

30

front. It is surprising that this method of 'mezzanine' planning was not more widely used in country houses, since it results in a small number of high-ceilinged rooms and a rather larger number of low-ceilinged ones, a most desirable result not so easily achieved by conventional planning. Apart from Kilcoltrim, Co. Carlow, I cannot readily recall another example of its use in an 18th-century country house (other than houses where the front and back halves are of different dates), but it reappears at Beechlawn (12, page 197) and in other small houses, including some in the Dublin suburbs, notably a group in Blackrock in or near Waltham Terrace.

The front elevation employs the familiar repertoire of tripartite doorcase, Venetian window and Diocletian window. It is raised on a plinth about 4 feet high which does not, for once, contain a basement. The walling is of very small squared stones: so small as almost to look like bricks. By this and other devices the house contrives to look larger than it is. How much, and how surprisingly, smaller it is than Dysart or Longfield may be verified by comparing their plans.

The entrance-hall has a Doric entablature over the door and side-lights, and an ingenious three-part composition on the inner wall, the right-hand section of which leads to the staircase (see 32, page 132). On the staircase-side there is more decoration in similar vein, but rectilinear, and the staircase has pierced and scrolled ends to the treads. Most of the doorcases have shouldered architraves, and some have pediments, and the drawing-room has a Rococo plaster ceiling and cove in a slightly provincial version of the manner of Robert West.

Summer Grove is only two miles from Mountmellick and eight from Portarlington, the principal Huguenot settlement in Ireland.

Elevation, section and plan by George Gossip

31

32

31 SUMMER GROVE
The rere elevation of this
building was originally quite
symmetrical and strictly
formal before the insertion
of two extra windows and
the addition of a box-like
porch. It shows a common,
and rather practical, disposition of the slopes and valleys,
similar to that to be seen at
the rere of, for example,
Colganstown, Co. Dublin.

32 SUMMER GROVE
The inner wall of the
entrance-hall, with decoration partly in carved wood
and partly in plaster. The
right-hand door gives access
to the staircase: that to the
left is a cupboard.

33

33 SUMMER GROVE
This decorative
wrought-iron lamp-
holder over the door is
a very rare feature in a
country house, though
not unlike similar
features in Dublin. In
Dublin, however, such
brackets are usually
attached to the railings
as, for example,
formerly at No. 45
Kildare Street.

34

34 SUMMER GROVE Two doorcases, drawn by George Gossip.

35

35-37 DYSART, *Delvin, Co. Westmeath.* Dysart was built in 1757 and designed by George Pentland (*floruit circa* 1750-70),[63] one of a family of architects of whom another designed Wilson's Hospital, a residential school about twelve miles away which still occupies its imposing original buildings of about the same date.

The plan of the house resembles that of Mount Hanover in the neighbouring county of Meath, except that the back rooms have round apses instead of polygons. The entrance-front of Mount Hanover faces west: that of Dysart faces east. Mount Hanover appears to be somewhat the earlier of the two. If, as seems likely, Richard Castle's Belvedere of about 1740 is the centre from which the Irish round-ended house began to spread, Dysart has a special place in being only seventeen years later, only twelve miles away, and by an identifiable architect.

Though simple and plain, Dysart is larger than it looks, as a comparison of its plan and elevation with that of, say, Ledwithstown, Co. Longford or Summer Grove, Co. Laois makes very clear. The ground falls abruptly at the back, so that the basement on the west side is fully above ground (compare Annaghlee, Co. Cavan in plates 55-59, pages 144-45). There are hardly any windows in the west wall, yet it boasts one of those hybrid pediment-gables so common in such situations. The ground-floor plan is elegantly modified on the first floor to accommodate a passage somewhat longer from north to south than the width of the hall below it, and the two stacks are carried on arches, as at Castletown Conolly. To

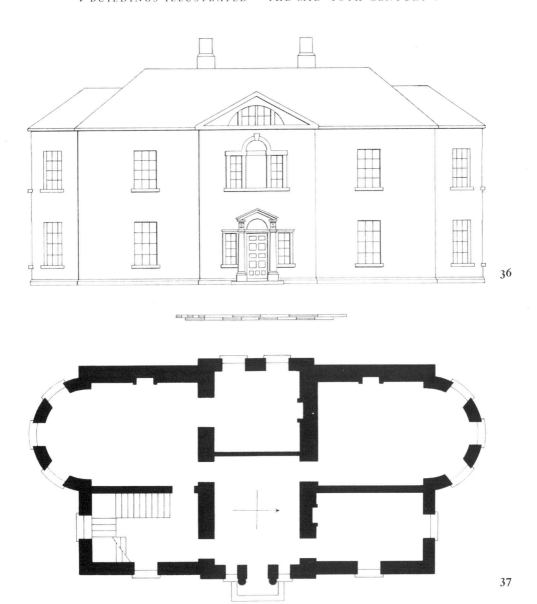

36

37

achieve this, the flues from the drawing and dining rooms are brought horizontally forward in the thickness of the dividing walls.

The doorcase, as with so many houses of the date, is a standard Dublin type, and above it comes the classic sequence of Venetian window and Diocletian window, the central section of the Venetian window being a niche in the manner familiar from Ballinter and other Richard Castle houses. The door has its original furniture, including a fine brass-mounted dug-out mahogany lock, similar to that illustrated on page 47.

Dysart remains in the possession of the family who built it.

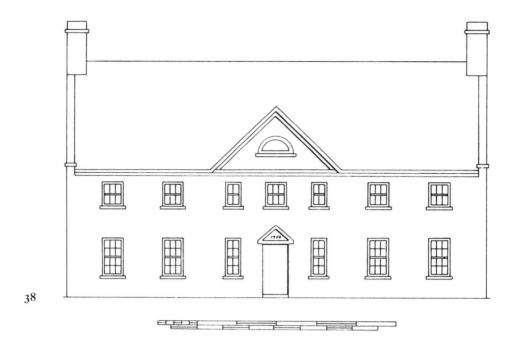

38

38 CARNMEEN, *Newry, Co. Down.* Though dated 1756, this house, with its steep 'floating' pediment and artless doorcase, has a very archaic flavour. It is quite closely paralleled by Ballystraw, Co. Wexford, and has also a clear relationship to the more developed category represented by Streamstown, Co. Offaly (76, page 153) and Clonbrogan, Co. Tipperary (75, page 153).
Elevation after the *Co. Down Archaeological Survey*

39

39 MOUNT GORDON, *Castlebar, Co. Mayo.* A modest but charming mid-18th-century house of the top-floor entry type, with the ubiquitous central half-octagon projection. One of the lean-to wings (compare Erindale, Co. Carlow in plate 5, page 192) has a niche, the other a window, and there are niches in the oblique faces of the central projection. It has a curiously close resemblance to the vaulted building called the 'Hell-Fire Club' at Montpelier in south County Dublin.

40

41

40 CLOGHER DEANERY,
Co. Tyrone. In this example
the unbroken roof over the
breakfront is awkward, and
may have been altered, nor is
the smooth plaster of the
breakfront happily contrasted
with the stripped rubble of
the rest of the front.

41 KILLININNY, *Tallaght,
Co. Dublin.* A large
comfortable 18th-century
farmhouse, now demolished,
but of a type still well
represented in the provinces.

42

42 LANDENSTOWN, *Sallins, Co. Kildare*. The massing of the main block with its open-bed pediment-gable recalls Ballykilcavan, Stradbally, Co. Laois. The great spread of the wings gives it an air of repose.

43-44 LISSENHALL, *Nenagh, Co. Tipperary*. This house, which belonged to the Otway family, is clearly from the same hand as Castle Otway in the same county, also ruined, and very similar except that it has a more conventional, pedimented, door-case. This channelled ashlar frontispiece at Lissenhall is elegant, accomplished and somewhat original, in allowing the impost-moulding to bind the doorway to the flanking windows. There is a channelled ashlar doorway in the base of the tower of the old Protestant church at Nenagh (facing the road to Lissenhall) which may have been done by the Otways.

45

45 BALRATH, *Kentstown, Co. Meath.* There are three Balraths in Meath: this is the southerly one, near the Slane road. The house seems to be mid-18th century, but has very late 18th-century plaster decoration.

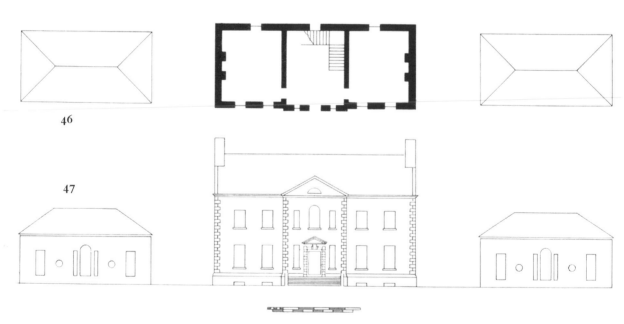

46

47

46-47 SHERWOOD PARK, *Ballon, Co. Carlow.* The wings of this house are agricultural buildings. The back (south) front of the main block is slate-hung: the entrance front faces due north. See also Dunstown (44, page 103).

48 FOREST BROOK, *Kilbroney, Co. Down*. Formerly a mill house, this building is a handsome specimen of a tripartite plan with narrow hall. The pediment, with coping instead of cornice, recalls that at Ballysallagh, Co. Kilkenny. The roof is almost imperceptibly sprocketed: if it were not so, it would be disagreeably perceptible.

49

49 CREEVAGHMORE, *Ballymahon, Co. Longford*. The door-case, in which the use of an architrave-moulding to define the stones flanking the keystone is without precedent, and very effective. The door has its original furniture. The timber open-well staircase is just inside the front door.

50

50 CREEVAGHMORE   The rere, towards the farmyard: it is remarkable how closely the plan of this house matches that given in the Reverend John Payne's *Twelve Designs for Country Houses,* published in Dublin in 1757 (see 15, page 56).

51

51 BERMINGHAM, *Tuam, Co. Galway.* A house with an unassuming exterior but an accomplished plan. The side-lights to the front door are spaced unusually wide, and the pattern of the fanlight, though simple, is unusual also.

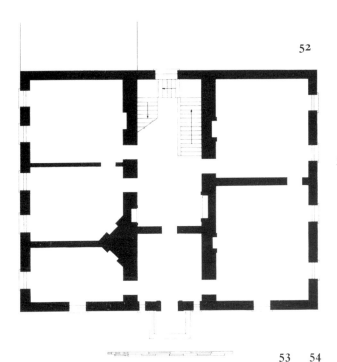

52

52 BERMINGHAM
Reticent in its elevations,
this house is a fine
example of a tripartite
plan on a fairly large scale,
with consistently high-
quality internal detailing
and decoration of the
mid-century.
Plan by William Garnerman

53   54

53   BOAKEFIELD, *Ballitore, Co. Kildare.* This building is similar in its proportions to
Ullard, Co. Kilkenny (63, page 114), but with the addition of wings which seem to
be contemporary. The designer was not overawed by the claims of symmetry, and
allowed the fenestration of the wings to take its natural course.

54   BOAKEFIELD The approach: the house still has a fine pair of rusticated gate-piers
topped with urns, and wickets hung from re-used columns.

57

55

56

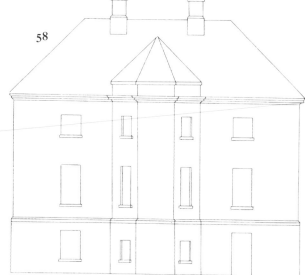

58

55-56 ANNAGHLEE, *Cootehill, Co. Cavan*. A red-brick house with tripartite plan, central bow, narrow hall, and staircase in half-octagon rere projection, attributed to Richard Castle and now almost completely destroyed.
Front elevation by David Griffin

57-58 ANNAGHLEE The rere elevation, showing how, as often, the basement level is the ground-level at the back. County Cavan, as witness Bellamont Forest, Annaghlee and Ballyhaise, has an unusual concentration of early brick houses.
Rere elevation by David Griffin

59

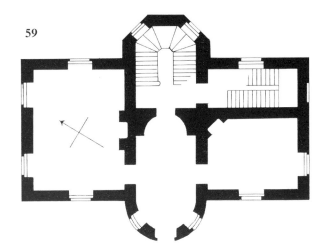

59 ANNAGHLEE
Annaghlee can be
regarded as in some
respects a slightly
expanded version of
Anneville, Co.
Westmeath (3-6, pages
117-19). The corner
fireplace in the south
room is conjectural, but
in other respects the
ruins provided enough
evidence to complete
the plan.
Plan by David Griffin

60

60 SYNGEFIELD, *Birr, Co. Offaly*. A quarter of this mid 18th-century house (on the
right of the façade) is now missing as a result of a fire. Originally it had Venetian
windows at both ends as well as in the middle. The Diocletian window in the basement is unusual.

61

62

61-62 ATHGOE, *Newcastle, Co. Dublin.* A mid 18th-century house beside the late-medi-aeval tower-house of the Lockes, who were still in occupation in the 1780s. The steep pediment-gable is an archaic feature. The doorcase is exactly like a Dublin doorcase of about 1760, but the two-leaf door is a country-house feature.

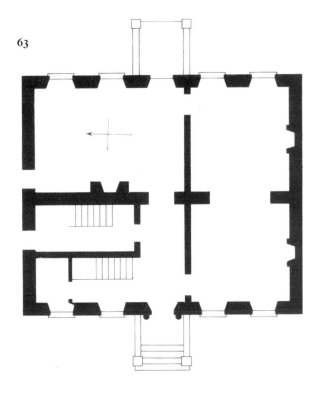

63

63 ATHGOE The flues from
the two fireplaces in the
eastern wall are led into
one of the two central
stacks. The provision of a
service stairs in a house of
this size is a little unusual.

64 THE SHRUBBERY,
Kilcock, Co. Kildare. The
central block of this house
dates from about 1760 and
contains plasterwork in the
style of Robert West; the
wings, lower but larger in
scale, were added *circa* 1800.

64

65

65-66 MILLMOUNT, *Maddoxtown, Co. Kilkenny*. This house was built for his own occupation by William Colles, the owner of the Kilkenny Marble Works which it adjoins, probably between 1760 and 1770. Among other activities, the works supplied the well-known black marble chimney-pieces to houses all over Ireland. *Plan and elevation after a survey by Jeremy Williams*

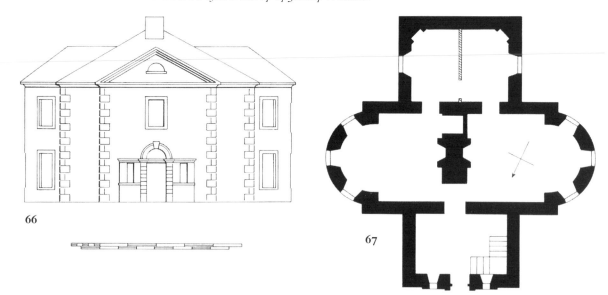

66

67

67 MILLMOUNT Millmount, an exceptionally formal house for its size, has a full basement which on the west (right) is above ground owing to the steep fall of the land to the river Nore.

148

68-69 SPRINGHILL,
Sleatygraigue (Carlow), Co. Laois. One step up in the scale from Killininny, Co. Dublin (41, page 137), Springhill has simple quadrant walls linking it to long simple barns acting as wings, as at Landenstown, Co. Kildare (42, page 138). One of the barns has been rebuilt.

The front hall has pretty plasterwork in the mid-18th-century style, and the house is probably of the third quarter. The table-top moulding of the front-door lintel, shown in plate 69, is worth noting. So is the cat in the bushes.

70

70 DROMISKIN GLEBE, now called ARDRONAN, *Co. Louth*. Built in 1766, according to Lewis's *Topographical Dictionary*, this pleasing rectory falls within the Reverend John Payne's *floruit* and within forty miles of where he lived. The doorcase of the building is similar to design No. 11 in his *Twelve Designs for Country Houses* (see plate 16, page 58), and altogether it seems likely that he designed it. The ground-floor windows are very slightly wider than those above them. The windows in the gable betray the position of the staircase.

71

72

71 CRANNAGH, *Templetuohy, Co. Tipperary*. A house of 1768 built on to a mediaeval cylindrical tower. Only the east end, here visible, has a bow: on the west end the ground-floor had formerly a Venetian window. The roof of the bow is a truncated half-cone with a lead flat on top.

72 CRANNAGH The mediaeval tower echoed by the curve of the 18th-century bow. In the 19th century the tower was given a steep polygonal slated hat.

73

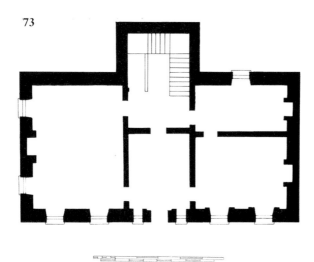

73 D U N M O R E , *Carrigans,
Co. Donegal.* Of the mid-
18th century, and perhaps
by Michael Priestley
(compare Port Hall, Co.
Donegal in 15, page
123), Dunmore has a
very similar plan to
Cuffesborough, Co.
Laois, which is dated
1770, except that at
Cuffesborough the stacks
are in the back wall
instead of in the end
walls, as here.
Plan by William Garnerman

74

74 CLOON, *Gort, Co. Galway.* A four-square gable-ended farmhouse with enough art
in the spacing of the openings to establish the irreducible Palladian minimum.
Compare Clonbrogan, Co. Tipperary in plate 75.

75 CLONBROGAN, *Fethard, Co. Tipperary*. With less in the way of polish than Piedmont, Co. Louth (47-49, page 105), this building has a similar arrangement of the windows, and sidelights to the door, much as at Cloon, Co. Galway (74, page 152) or at Streamstown, Kinnitty, Co. Offaly. Here, at Clonbrogan, the lower part of the back wall is obscured by a later lean-to, but there is evidence for an earlier, higher, lean-to, and the single window now visible in the north wall is high up in the centre. The notched brick cornice is apparently original, since it occurs elsewhere in an 18th-century context.

75

76

76 STREAMSTOWN, *Kinnitty, Co. Offaly*. The resemblance to Cloon, Co. Galway, and Clonbrogan, Co. Tipperary, is apparent. It is about the same distance (forty miles) from each of them, and they are about sixty miles apart: but the distribution of the type is no doubt even wider, and indeed the 'Manor House', Tollymore, Co. Down, for all the grandeur of its appellation, differs from these only in having a simple semicircular fanlight over the door.

77

77–82 COLGANSTOWN, *Newcastle, Co. Dublin.* Not a great deal is known about the date or original ownership of Colganstown. It appears to have been built by a family variously spelt as Yates or Yeats, who had a house in Sackville Street (now O'Connell Street, Dublin) in the 1760s, and owned also Moone House in County Kildare, a house itself not without interest. The Knight of Glin has made a good case[45] for regarding it as part of the *oeuvre* of Nathaniel Clements, a politician and banker turned architect, who was born in 1705. He was a political associate of the great Luke Gardiner of Henrietta Street, who speaks of him as an 'architect' as early as 1744.

One thing is certain: that Colganstown belongs with Clements's own house Woodville, with his other house (later transformed as the Viceregal Lodge), with Williamstown, Co. Kildare, with Newberry Hall, with Belview, and probably also

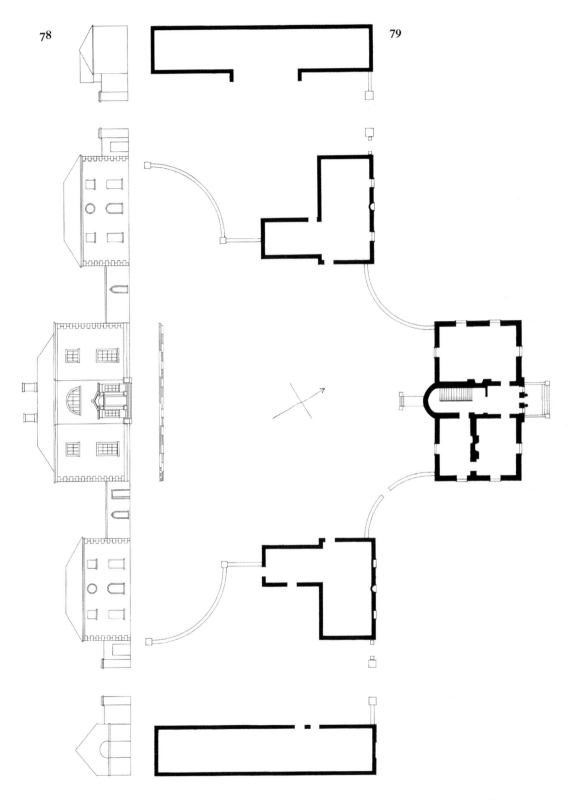

78

79

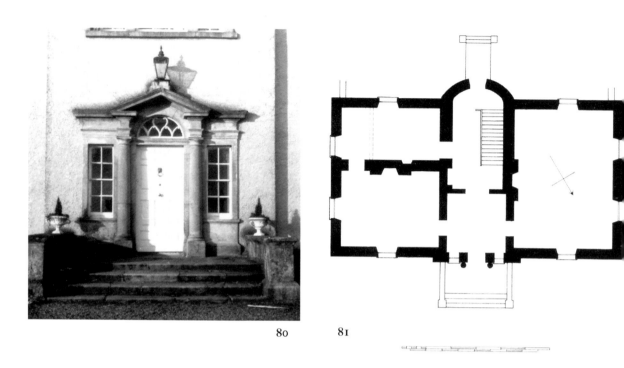

80   81

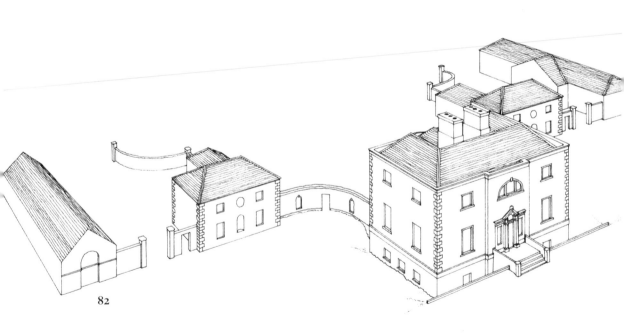

82

with Lodge Park, Straffan. It is impossible yet to say where it belongs in the series, but the character of its internal decoration, admirable stucco decoration in the style of Robert West, suggests a date in the 1760s.

It is a 'Sabine farm' in the fullest sense: a mere ten miles from the centre of Dublin, though in a part of the county little visited to this day. And, of course, it is an exemplar of the 'economic layout' in its most elaborate and elegant form.

The independence of plan and elevation in the 18th century is well illustrated by the fact that whereas the elevations of Colganstown and Newberry Hall are virtually identical, the Newberry staircase is at the side while that of Colganstown is at the back. At Colganstown more of the available space is given to the rooms flanking the hall and staircase, so that the stacks are perceptibly closer together than at Newberry. In most other respects, however, the Colganstown elevation seems to me to be the better of the two. The window-architraves are slenderer and more elegant: the lightly handled cornice suits the mood: for my part I do not miss the pediment and parapet, while the touch of fantasy in the glazing of the doorcase, entirely absent from Newberry, as it is absent also from the pattern-book plate from which it derives, shows how much depends on the execution and, at this date, no doubt on the inspiration of individual craftsmen on the job. It is even possible that the close similarity between the Newberry and Colganstown elevations is an indication that they are by two different architects, and not, as has hitherto been assumed, by the same one.

If both Colganstown and Kilcarty, Co. Meath are regarded as 'hobby' farms belonging to gentlemen living in Dublin, there is a distinction to be drawn between the types they represent. In one case (Colganstown and its relatives) the gentleman could look out of his front windows, or his back windows, without actually seeing the farmyards. In the other case (Kilcarty, Clooncallick, Creevaghmore *et al*) he would see the farmyard if he looked out of his back windows. In modern terms there is an analogy with the man who lets his hobby – hi-fi, model engineering, vintage cars – invade the living-room, and the man whose wife insists that it be confined to a workshop at the bottom of the garden.

The internal decoration of Colganstown is entirely metropolitan in quality. The small square hall is groin-vaulted with delicate plaster enrichment: the doors are of beautiful pale mahogany. The staircase-hall ceiling has, in its wandering Rococo. design, elongated versions of the cornucopia so frequently seen on the Dublin bookbindings of the 1760s, while, over the staircase window, presides a splendidly animated Chinese dragon, scaly wings outstretched, and his tail piercing the egg-and-dart moulding at the base of the cornice to emerge and recurve again, stabbing the plasterwork. Elsewhere the birds of the west school are ubiquitous in high relief, with baskets of fruit and flowers.

There is some doubt about how much of the economic layout was built as designed. The north pavilion is more cheaply finished than the southern: but the evidence of the 1837 Ordnance map is contradictory.

Drawings by Derry O'Connell

83 COLGANSTOWN The central block, facing north-east.

84 COLGANSTOWN The rere elevation: the central bow, rather too narrow to be graceful, contains the staircase.

85 NEWBERRY HALL, *Carbury, Co. Kildare*. Built, probably by Nathaniel Clements, for Viscount Harberton in the 1760s, the façade of this house is identical with that of Colganstown, Co. Dublin save for the pediment and parapet, and for being of brick. The windows visible in the return wall to the right are those of the staircase. The wings with their half-octagon bays are very unusual in Ireland.

86

86 NEWBERRY HALL The central block: the stacks are perceptibly farther apart than those of Colganstown.

87

88

87 **BELVIEW**, *Oldcastle, Co. Meath.* With sweeps and wings forming an economic layout, this unusually small house of about 1765 has been attributed to Nathaniel Clements.[41] The staircase is in the bow-projection to the right or west.

88 **SPRINGHILL**, *Moneymore, Co. Derry.* Though it seems to have started life as a late 17th-century house and contains a handsome early 18th-century staircase beside a winding stair in an irregularly round casing, Springhill's present appearance was given to it in about 1765 when the wings, with their semi-octagonal fronts, were added, giving it a resemblance to Edenmore, Co. Donegal. The curvilinear-gabled agricultural wings, which form the deep forecourt, seem to be early 18th-century and recall Shannongrove, Co. Limerick.

89

89 CASTLE COR, *Ballymahon, Co. Longford.* This mid-to-late-18th-century house seems to have been originally an octagon with four equal projecting arms. Some time in the early 19th century a quite conventional house-front was built on to it: this is now obscured by a slightly wider house-front added early in the present [twentieth] century, in the 18th-century manner. It resembles Clemenswerth in Lower Saxony, which is a few years earlier. *Drawing by Michael Craig*

THE LATE-18TH CENTURY
1770-1800

I

1–3   KILCARTY , *Kilmessan, Co. Meath*. More perhaps than any other building, Kilcarty occupies a pivotal position on the frontier between the farmhouse and the mansion. Its central block, deprived of its wings, would simply be another gable-ended farmhouse: beautifully proportioned indeed, as are many others, but absolutely plain and proclaiming its humble affinities by the protrusion of its gable-stacks, the absence of a cornice and its unassuming rough-cast lime-plaster finish. Even its modest doorcase must have been a little old-fashioned by the time it was built.

     The low two-bay wings, their front walls in the same plane without a break, are still firmly within the farmhouse tradition. Nor is it extraordinary for the farmyard to lie behind the house, as it does here (see plate 2, page 165). The extreme formality of the treatment, however, with the pedimented fronts of the farm-buildings rising above and behind the shallow curved sweeps, and the centrally placed barn at the back balancing the mass of the house itself, is another matter. The total effect is one of bland serenity.

     Kilcarty is one of the very few houses of its date which have a known architect. It was designed by Thomas Ivory of Dublin (*circa* 1720-86) for Dr George Cleghorn, professor of anatomy, who died in 1789, and was probably built about 1770-1780. Considering the great difference in purpose, scale and finish between the two buildings, it is remarkable how close the conception of Kilcarty is to that of Ivory's design for the King's Hospital (Blue Coat) School.[64] The everyday dress and vernacular

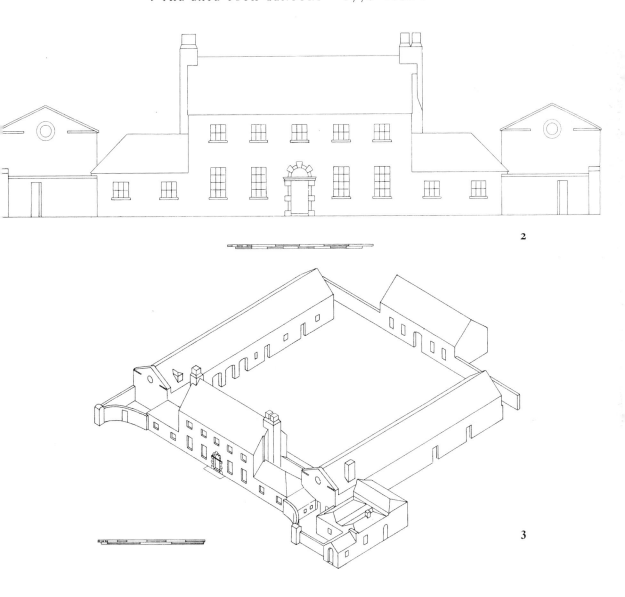

2

3

affinities of Kilcarty cloak a design of exceptional subtlety and refinement.

It is uncertain whether the low buildings at the north end of the main front are original or later: it is quite possible that having made his grand symmetrical statement, Ivory was happy enough to add, as it were, a coda in the same vein. There is one characteristic of the Kilcarty elevation which does not appear in the Blue Coat School nor, as far as I know, elsewhere. In sum, it is that at no point are the limiting corners of the major masses of the composition allowed to show themselves at ground level. In technical language, some very surprising tricks are played with the 'inflexion' of the parts. One would expect, for example, that the difference in weight between the two-storey house and the one-storey wings would be expressed by a small set-back of the plane of the wings, as it always is in such conjunctions. When

Ivory broke this elementary rule, he can only have done so on purpose.

In a different way he conceals the outer terminations of these low wings, by making the shallow sweep-walls overlap them by a small but significant amount, instead of setting them back by a foot or two, as nearly everybody else did. We are not allowed to see the corners of these wings reach the ground, though we can see the top foot or so of the corners, above the sweep-walls; so that with this and the roofs to guide us we know how far they extend. Finally, and most obviously, the pedimented stable-ends seem to float above and behind the foreground, and we can only infer that they, in turn, overlap the low wings, because we cannot see their bases.

It is an irony of the most piquant kind that this manneristic essay should have been carried out in the idiom of the whitewashed farmhouse. To find a parallel we must look at the mannerism of James Gandon's very private games at the double courtyard – equestrian and agricultural – of the Carriglas stables.

To whom, I sometimes ask myself, do architects speak? To themselves? To their own subconscious? Hardly, in this case, to Dr Cleghorn or his successors in title. For two hundred years this building has been standing, with its message on its face; and only after thirty years of (as I thought) intimate knowledge of it, have I noticed the facts set down above. The moral, I suppose, is that when real thought has gone into the making of any building, there is no limit to the number of times one can, and should, look at it.

4   KILCARTY A corner of the farmyard, as it was before recent alterations. The lean-to passage ran right across from wing to wing, with continuous roofing, and could be reached by a door under the staircase window.

4

5

5 WILTON, *Urlingford, Co. Kilkenny*. A typical mid-to-late 18th-century house with a central half-octagon. Now regrettably derelict.

6

6-7 WHITE CASTLE, *Inishowen, Co. Donegal.* A late 18th-century house with shallow bows on the ends and half-octagons in the centre of each front. The cramped upper storey has parallels in the neighbouring town of Raphoe.

7

8   B E L L E V U E , *Finglas, Co. Dublin.* A late 18th-century house with bows at front and back, and at one end. This is the back, where the bow is square at ground level and octagonal higher up.

9   K I L D U F F , *Daingean (Philipstown), Co. Offaly.* Apparently of the late 18th century, to judge by its joinery, Kilduff has a number of curious features. The main doorcase is like a Dublin doorcase of the 1760s, but the side (basement) doorcase to the yard is of comparable quality. One of the first-floor corner fireplaces is balanced almost over a void, and the long wide arch behind joins the two stacks. The walls are unusually thick for a house of its size and date. The roofing structure is exceptional: from each corner of the house a massive principal truss with collar only (no tie) is placed diagonally with its inward end resting on the mass of masonry forming the stacks, and between these four trusses there are nothing but light common rafters. There is of course a central well. In the north-west corner of the house (top-right) an unfinished room of some pretension, with small under-square windows, occupies part of the roof-space, and is reached by the four steps from the first-floor landing.

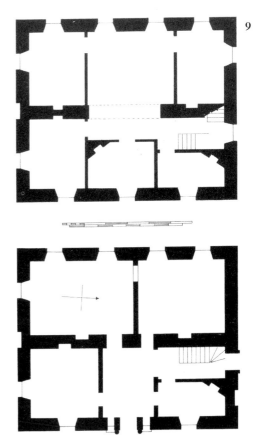

9

10

10 BALLYNURE, *Grange Con, Co. Wicklow*. A courtyard farmstead of more than usual
formality. It is probably not as old as the massive doorcase would suggest but it is
clearly not long for this world, which is a pity.

11 EDENMORE, *Stranorlar, Co. Donegal*. Plan of layout. This late 18th-century building
is an example of the 'end-on' type of wings, in this case more symmetrical in elevation than in reality.
Plan by William Garnerman

12 LODGE PARK, *Straffan, Co. Kildare*. An extreme example of the 'stretched' layout
exemplified, among large houses, by Russborough. There are five blocks altogether,
that to the farthest left being hidden by the trees. The house is credited to Nathaniel
Clements and was built in 1775-77.

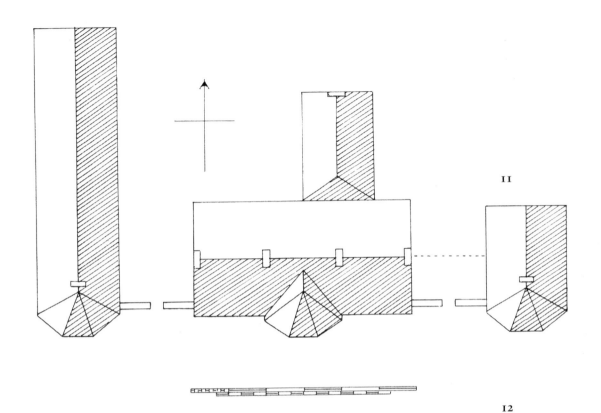

II

12

13   MARLAY, *Co. Dublin.* The frontispiece of the late 18th century house of the La Touche family of bankers. The urn is obviously derivative from those on the Custom House in Dublin.

13

14

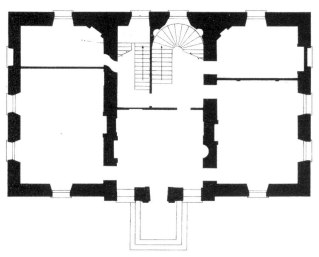

14-15 CASTLE FFRENCH, *Ahascragh, Co. Galway*. Dating probably from the 1770s, this house has a very similar plan to Bonnetstown, Co. Kilkenny, forty years earlier and seventy miles away (see plate 31, page 93). A resemblance to Bonnetstown is also apparent in the back elevation of Castle Ffrench (see 15) where the twin central windows are those of the two staircases.
Drawing by William Garnerman

15

16

17

16 BOWEN'S COURT, *Farahy, Co. Cork.* The doorcase of a house built in 1776 and credited to Isaac Rothery. The cornice and pediment are too light in section for their position.

17 BOWEN'S COURT The dining-room with its original Kilkenny marble fireplace and grate. The house was demolished in 1961.

18

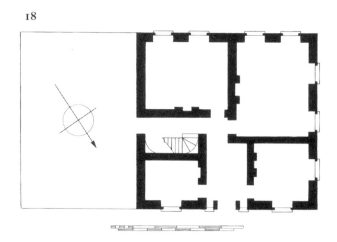

18 NEWPARK, *Ballymote, Co. Sligo.* This house quite likely belongs to the last quarter of the 18th century. The 'swastika' type plan is found also at Oakfield, Co. Donegal, originally built as the Deanery of Raphoe. Four rectangles are arranged in a square, leaving a small square in the middle. Oakfield is perhaps fifty years earlier.
Drawing by William Garnerman

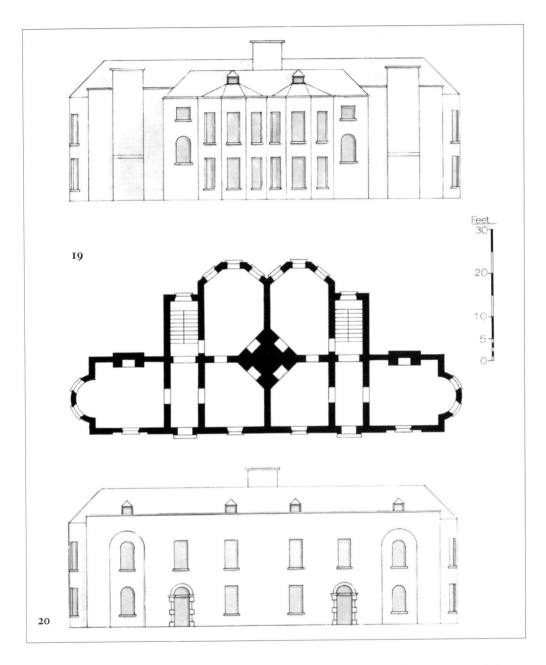

Feet
30
20
10
5
0

19

20

19-20 WINDY ARBOUR, *Dundrum, Co. Dublin.* Windy Arbour quite probably belongs to the last quarter of the 18th century, and among the earliest examples of the semi-detached layout in the country. The provision of a single massive stack is an archaic feature, found also in pairs of Dublin town houses. There is a plan and elevation of a pair of semi-detached houses among the Vanbrugh drawings at Elton Hall (No. 115). *Surveyed by Mark Leslie*

21 **PRIOR PARK**, *Borrisokane, Co. Tipperary.* The unusually fine proportions and the subtle spacing of the windows, together with the strong cornice, raise this house well above the usual run of houses with which it is superficially comparable. It was built between 1779 and 1786 and closely resembles Johnstown two miles away, now in ruins.

21

22

22-23 **VERNON MOUNT**, *Douglas, Co. Cork.* A remarkable geometric house of the late 18th-century, built by an unknown architect for Sir Henry Hayes. The slightly cambered window-heads would be remarkable at this date (*circa* 1784) anywhere but in County Cork, where they lingered on much longer than elsewhere. Sir Henry Hayes, the builder, was transported to Australia for abduction, but the defensive front door grille seen in plate 23 dates from our less peaceful times.

23

24

25

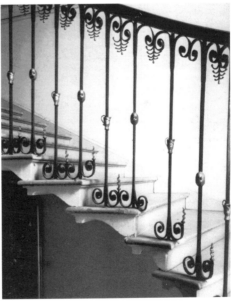

24-25 VERNON MOUNT The upstairs lobby: architecturally-treated upstairs central lobbies are characteristic of many larger Irish houses, but not so often found in one of this size. The paintings are by Nathaniel Grogan. A detail of the staircase at Vernon Mount is shown in plate 25.

26

26-28 R O K E B Y   H A L L , *Dunleer, Co. Louth*. The north (entrance) front of the house built for Richard Robinson, Archbishop of Armagh, in the years following 1785, probably by Thomas Cooley (1740–84) and certainly with the participation of Francis Johnston (1760–1829). Both in elevation and in plan it is related to Lucan House, and in plan also to Mount Kennedy. James Wyatt, Michael Stapleton, Richard Johnston and even Sir William Chambers are involved in a complex tale which may never be fully unravelled. Rokeby is more remarkable for the beauty of its detail than for its overall expression which has, however, suffered by the loss of its glazing-bars. Details of the staircase and external steps at Rokeby are given in plates 27 and 28.

27

28

29

29 DERRYMORE,
Camlough, Co. Armagh. Built
before 1787 by Isaac Corry,
in the form of a deep U–
plan, Derrymore displays
fanciful Gothic features
such as may be seen at
Luggala, Co. Wicklow,
Lissanoure, Co. Antrim and
Jenkinstown, Co. Kilkenny:
here crowned with a most
attractive roof of thatch.
The far ends of the U
terminate in shallow bows.
There was a good early
19th-century entrance-hall,
demolished by the present
owners.

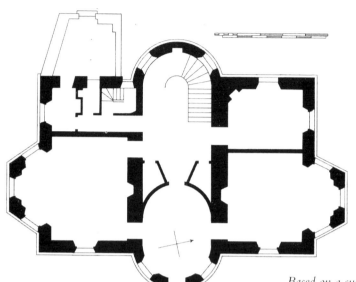

30 LONGFIELD, *Goold's Cross, Co. Tipperary*. The joinery of this house suggests a date fairly late in the 18th century. The plan-form is closely related to that of Dromard, Co. Limerick (59, page 112) and Lisdonagh, Co. Galway (see 31-33, page 181) which may be later.

Based on a survey by Peter Ferguson & Associates

30

31

32

31-32 LISDONAGH, *Headford, Co. Galway.*
Similar in plan to Longfield, but without
the end-bows, Lisdonagh probably dates
from the 1790s. The hall is oval, with walls
painted with an Ionic order and figures in
grisaille, and behind it the staircase is
partly contained in a three-sided projection. The two massive stacks are unusual
in emerging so deep in plan from the
roof, and so rapidly diminishing, like the
funnel of the *Chusan.*

33

The house is flanked on the right by
a little detached Palladian pavilion with a
tripartite window on one side and a niche
on the side facing the house (see plate
32). If there was ever another such
pavilion on the right-hand side it had
gone by the 6-inch Ordnance Survey of
1837. Flowerhill, Tynagh, Co. Galway also
has detached pyramidally roofed pavilions.

33 LISDONAGH Detail of the doorcase: the door and the glazing of the fanlight are
modern, as is the Disney-style lantern supported by the magnificent heraldic bird.

34

34-36 E M S W O R T H, *Malahide, Co. Dublin*. Emsworth was built by James Gandon (1743–1823) for Mr J. Woodmason, who seems to have been a wholesale stationer of 129 Lower Abbey Street. His preliminary drawings are dated 1794, and differ a little, as drawings always do, from the house as built. A little subsequent alteration has taken place, but not much. Of all the villa designs which Gandon is known to have made, this is the only one which survives as a building in substantially intact form.

Gandon's drawings are not suitable for reproduction. The drawing given here in 35 is a compromise, being in part derived from his, and in part adjusted to conform with the existing structure. The principal differences are these: the first-floor windows, circular in his drawing, are given as rectangles and were probably so carried out. The mutules of the porch, and the dentils of the main pediment, do not appear on his drawing but are present in the building and are so characteristic of Gandon that they must be original. The elevated roof in the south (left) wing is shown as executed, though Gandon does not show it in his elevation, it is implied in his section. There is some uncertainty about the original ground-levels. Otherwise I believe that the drawing given in 35 fairly represents the house as Gandon left it. It is six miles north-east of Dublin and thus a very fair example of a successful merchant's villa.

Gandon did not, as a general rule, borrow much from Irish models. He began, at least, by believing that there was nothing in Ireland worth serious consideration.

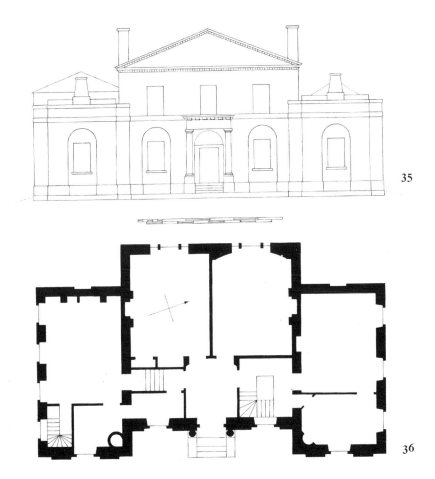

35

36

Yet here it seems that we find him using the low overlapping wings whose ancestry goes back through Buncrana Castle, Lismore and Waringstown to Jigginstown in the 1630s.[65] We know that he knew Jigginstown at first hand.

The chimney-urns on the wings of Emsworth are very Gandonian: close relatives of those intended for Carriglas.[66] The left or south wing contains the kitchen and the north wing a study and reception-room: the exact opposite of what would now be thought appropriate. From the outset it was intended to sink the kitchen floor below the general level, and to fit in another storey above it, to be reached no doubt by the staircase in that wing. If this staircase ever existed it has now gone, and access to the rooms above the kitchen is by a few steps down from the upper storey of the main block.

The grey marble chimney-pieces of the dining and drawing rooms are of the utmost severity, and a severe reticence is the keynote of the whole house, both inside and out. Evidently Mr Woodmason the merchant's taste was the equal of any fine gentleman's: or perhaps he wisely did as his architect told him to.

37

37 CHURCH HILL, *Fenit, Co. Kerry*. Although apparently originally the glebe-house (and Lewis's *Topographical Dictionary* says the glebe-house was built in 1741) this house, with its late doorway and tripartite window, looks more like 1800, while the large central bow on the seaward side can hardly be as early as the 1740s in Kerry. The unusual way in which the roof over the breakfront is made to die into the main ridge under cover of the stacks may indicate a remodelling.

38

38 BALLYOWEN COTTAGE, *Lucan, Co. Dublin.* The single-storey addition to an earlier, plain, house of *circa* 1800 has elegantly swept slating.

39

39-41 GALTRIM, *Summerhill, Co. Meath.* Galtrim is probably the best of Francis Johnston's smaller houses. It is fairly closely dateable, since the Honourable and Reverend Vesey Dawson for whom it was built, married the sister of Blayney Townley of the nearby Townley Hall (Johnston's best large house) in 1793, and was Rector of Galtrim from 1794 to 1806, and the Coade-stone lions carry the date 1802. The design can in some lights be regarded as a hybrid between Kilcarty, Co. Meath and Emsworth, Co. Dublin by Ivory and Gandon respectively. Kilcarty is only four miles away, and Johnston must be presumed to have known it, as he must certainly also have known Emsworth (the plan of which he copied very closely for another house: see 11, page 196).

The north or entrance front of Galtrim is shown in plate 39. The relationship between the main block and the wings recalls Kilcarty, and so, even more forcibly, does the role of the small quadrants which flank them. The central bow at the back is a well-established Irish feature, and one which Gandon used in the unexecuted design for Carriglas, where, as at Slane, a large house not far from Galtrim, it was

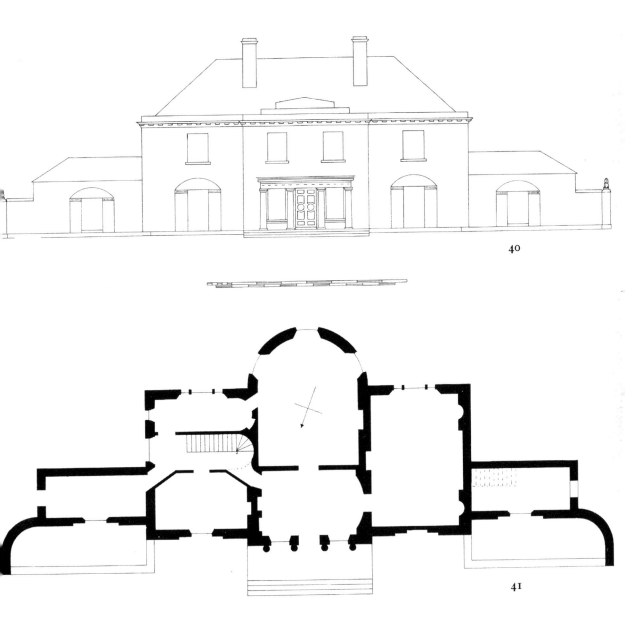

40

41

to accommodate a round room. At Galtrim the Gandon influence is to be seen in the shallow curve which forms one end of the entrance-hall (compare the entrance-hall and the drawing-room of Emsworth), in the setting of the windows in recessed planes contained by shallow arches, and in the tall tripartite windows in the garden-front, also as at Emsworth. An earlier designer would almost certainly have resolved the duality of the upper storey by placing a niche between the central windows. Here, as at Ballynagall, Co. Westmeath, Johnston scorned to use such an expedient, and here, also as at Ballynagall, he tied the centre of the ground storey together with an order: at Ballynagall an Ionic portico, at Galtrim an engaged Doric frontispiece of similar proportions. Ballynagall is at once obviously more expensive, and weaker. The ornament of the door-panels first appears in Ireland in the work of Davis Ducart in the 1760s, but in this case it seems to be a re-introduction via William Playfair, who worked at Townley Hall before Johnston. It is again very common in the early 19th century.

The house, colour-washed a pleasant shade of ochre, has been hardly at all altered. The planning is ingenious but, in its original form, inconvenient in that the kitchen under the dining-room can be reached only by the lower flights of the single staircase in the other end of the block. The approach from the entrance-hall to the staircase is much more elegant than it appears on the plan. The decoration, in which much elegant play is made with almost imperceptibly recessed planes, recessed by less than half an inch in both ceilings and walls, is of the coolest kind imaginable.

Johnston's debt to Emsworth is in some ways even more evident in his design for the Private Secretary's lodge in the Phoenix Park (see 11, page 196), which is a paraphrase of the Emsworth plan, complete with low overlapping wings, and a very Irish touch in the gathering of all the flues into a single central stack.

THE EARLY 19TH
CENTURY
1800–1835

1 FORT SHANNON, *Glin, Co. Limerick.* The north front, facing the river Shannon. The curved wall to the right is the beginning of the long sinuous wall which bounds the yard on the west, and has lean-to structures inside it. A pair of chimney-pots serving the two-storey wing are just visible above the cow whose head appears in profile.

2 FORT SHANNON The north wing is single-storey (see 1) and the south-east wing is of two storeys with the same eaves-height. The outline, with its numerous bows, is extremely picturesque, but it was all built at the same time, no doubt by an amateur designer.

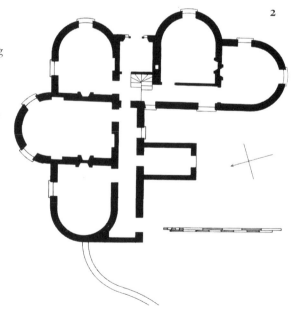

3 THE SEXTON'S HOUSE, *Bagenalstown, Co. Carlow.* Unusually severe and scholarly in treatment for so small a building, this house may perhaps be by William Robertson of Kilkenny. The use of a Greek Doric order *in antis* in this way is paralleled at a very remarkable house of geometric plan at Rath, near Tullow, about fourteen miles away.

4 BALLYMORE, *Lawrencetown, Co. Galway.* A house of about 1800 with a shallow bow-front and wide eaves, built on to a well-preserved tower-house.

3

4

5

5   E R I N D A L E , *Carlow, Co. Carlow*. This remarkable red-brick house, probably of
about 1800, combines a common double bow-fronted plan with the ubiquitous
'Venetian' windows, but this time flavoured with a 'gothick' idiom. It is uncertain
whether the flat relieving-arches (visible in the left-hand bow) indicate a change of
mind or a later alteration. The elaborate glazing of the fanlight seems to be original,
and so do the opening casements in the windows of the upper storey; but that in the
heads of the ground-floor windows looks a little later. There is a projection at the
back of the house which may be an older, smaller house, and on the public road is a
stone barn adorned with obelisks on balls, prettily framed slits, and blind quatrefoils,
which belongs to the house and must be an expression of the same off-beat taste as
the house itself. The lean-to wings with their niches are paralleled as far away as
Mount Gordon in County Mayo (39, page 136). There used to be some gothick
Venetian windows in Wexford Street, Dublin.

6

6   D E L A F O R D , *Firhouse, Co. Dublin.* A single-storey frontispiece added by Alderman
Bermingham in about 1800 to an earlier three-storey house, originally an inn called
Clandarigg. The large rooms flanking the hall have bow-ends (now destroyed).

7

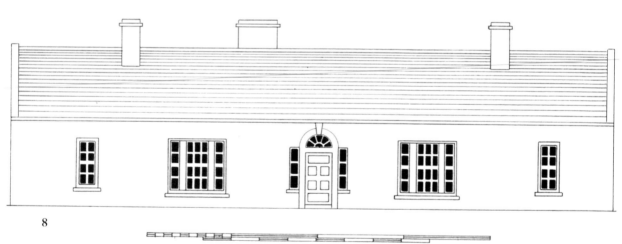

8

7   BEECH PARK, *Esker, Co. Dublin.* A house of about 1800, unusual in its asymmetry

8   BALLYGOWAN COTTAGE, *Claremorris, Co. Mayo.* Elevation of the entrance (north) front. Of about 1800, and without basement, this house has a T-plan, the stem (south) of the T being of two storeys with the same eaves height: compare Fort Shannon, Co. Limerick (1, page 190).

9

9   BLOOMFIELD,
Rathfarnham, Co. Dublin. An
early 19th-century double
bow-fronted house, typical of
many and now demolished.

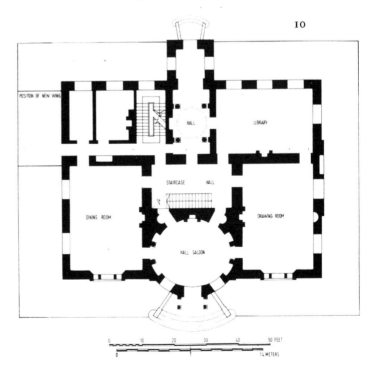

10

10   CASTLEGAR, *Ahascragh,
Co. Galway.* Built by Sir
Richard Morrison
(1767–1849) in 1807, this
house displays features typical
of Morrison's villa planning:
from the elliptical hall with its
inset columns and the small
back hall with its dome carried
on columns, to the triple
windows on the entrance
front. The back half of the
house contains one more
storey than the front half.
Drawing by John O'Connell

11

11 PHOENIX PARK Francis Johnston's unexecuted design for a Lodge for the Private Secretary, signed and dated 1808. It will be noticed how closely the plan derives from that of Gandon's Emsworth (compare the plan of Emsworth given in 35, page 183) and how all the flues are, as so often, brought to a single central stack. An engraving of this design, with the mouldings coarsened, was reproduced without acknowledgement in William Stitt's *Practical Architect's Ready Assistant,* published in Dublin in 1819.

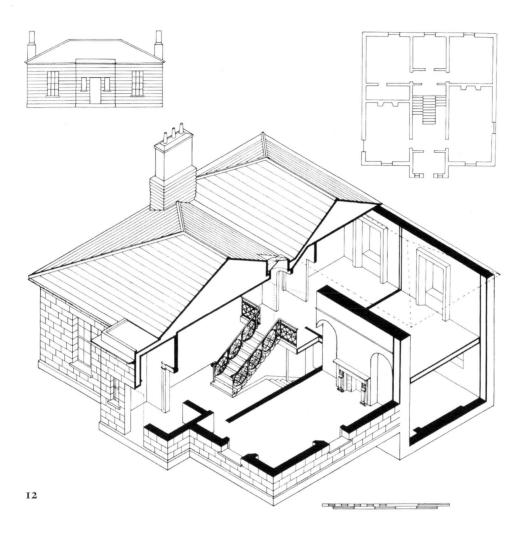

12

12 BEECHLAWN, *Rathgar, Dublin*. Said to have been built about 1816, and credited by its late owner Colm Ó Lochlainn to Francis Johnston (1760–1829), this small house in the suburbs of Dublin is faced with granite ashlar. As this isometric section shows, it is a single storey high in front (without basement) and two storeys high at the back, the lower storey being a semi-basement. It embodies on a smaller scale the principle used at Summer Grove, Co. Laois (26-34, pages 129-133), but with greater formal display, since the central single-flight staircase leads to a landing lighted by an overhead dome. From this landing open the bedrooms, of moderate size and height, easy to heat. A pair of parallel flights lead to the semi-basement kitchens. The two front reception-rooms are lofty and spacious for so small a house. A similar principle was used in the very varied, yet carefully harmonised, houses on the Waltham Terrace, Blackrock development of the Pembroke Estate in Couny Dublin, in the 1830s, by an unknown but very resourceful designer.

13

13 H A L S T O N , *Moyvore, Co. Westmeath*, of which the garden front is shown here, was
built *circa* 1820, has a tripartite plan and is approximately square. There is consequently
a deep wide hall, with the staircase at the north end of it (shown centrally in this
photograph). The real 'back' of the house, meaning the place where the kitchen door
is, is to the left in this picture.

14

15

14 HALSTON The south
(entrance) front: the effective
'back' of the house is the
façade to the right, where
the basement is virtually
above ground.

15 ST FINTAN'S, *Howth,
Co. Dublin.* A detached
suburban house of about
1820 with a very correct, but
rather frigid, 'Tower of the
Winds' porch.

16

16 ANNESBROOK, *Duleek, Co.
Louth.* The treatment of the ground-
floor windows in this house is
similar to that at Galtrim, Co. Meath
(39, page 186). The portico and the
'banqueting-room' to the left are
said to have been added in 1821 in
anticipation of the visit of George
IV on his way to visit Lady
Conyngham at Slane.

17 ANNESBROOK The portico: the
supposition that it is an addition is
strengthened by the discrepancy
between the intercolumniations and
the width of the doorway.

17

18

18 KILDEVIN, *Street, Co. Westmeath*. This house bears the date 1833 and the name Robert Sproule, incised over the door. The Sproules were a family of architects, and this may have been one of them. The central bow continues back through the plan as a high balustraded attic and emerges as another similar bow at the back, facing the farmyard. The plan is not known but is probably very interesting: a late fruit of the geometric tradition.

NOTES

1   Desmond Guinness and William Ryan, *Irish Houses and Castles* London 1971. Belvedere appears both in that book and in this.

2   E. E. Evans, *Irish Heritage* Dundalk 1942, often reprinted, and numerous learned papers. See also Kevin Danaher, (Caoimhín Ó Danachair) numerous learned papers and, most recently, *Ireland's Vernacular Architecture* Cork 1975.

3   Many of Francis Place's drawings are in the National Gallery of Ireland. See also *Journal of the Royal Society of Antiquaries of Ireland* LXII (1932), i sqq.

4   See H. G. Leask, *Irish Castles* Dundalk 1941, p. 90 for a reconstruction drawing.

5   See Maurice Craig in Howard Colvin and John Harris (eds), *The Country Seat* London 1970, pp. 36 sqq.

6   H. G. Leask, *op cit* figs 91 and 92.

7   Plans by D. Waterman in *Studies in Building History* (ed E. M. Jope) London 1961, which contains other useful 17th-century plans by the same hand.

8   There are exceptions such as Knockgraffon, Co. Tipperary and Brazeel, Co. Dublin (see p. 55), and of course also the larger houses such as Portumna, though in most of even these the staircase was in a corner tower.

9   *Irish Georgian Society Bulletin* October-December 1973: elevation by David Griffin, but the plan on the same page is not of Cuffesborough.

10 Maurice Craig and the Knight of Glin, *Irish Architectural Drawings* exhibition catalogue 1965, No. 33 illustrated: late 17th-century design for Castle Coole.

11 Illustrated in Maurice Craig and the Knight of Glin, *Ireland Observed* Cork 1970, p. 53. The plan has since been recovered by John O'Connell from the ruins.

12 E. E. Evans, *Irish Heritage* p. 59, and K. Danaher, *Ireland's Vernacular Architecture* passim e.g. pp. 26, 27.

13 In E. M. Jope (ed). *Studies in Building History* London 1961, pp 251-74, especially 260, 261, 262.

14 There is a survey of Mosstown in Parks and Monuments Division of the Office of Public Works, Dublin.

15 See H. G. Leask in *Studies in Building History* pp. 243-50.

16 E. M. Jope in *Ulster Journal of Archaeology* XXI, 1958 pp. 109-12.

17 With a pair of large windows, as clearly seen in the back view of Bonnetstown in de Breffny and ffolliott, *Houses of Ireland* 1975, p. 10, or, less elegantly, in page 173 in this book.

18 See the Knight of Glin in *The Country Seat* pp. 185-91, where Gandon's drawings are reproduced.

19 *Country Life* 24 and 31 May 1973.

20 Plan in D. Waterman, *Studies in Building History* p. 273 where, however, it is called 'Cregg'. The door shown in the back wing is mistaken, and so is the statement on p. 274 that

there is no indication of a stair. The 'ghost' on the inner face of the wing wall is still quite clear. Though with the same eaves-height, the back wing has three storeys plus attic while the front block has two storeys plus attic.

21   There was at Killester, Co. Dublin, an unusually beautiful small early 18th-century single-storey house with a timber cornice, a steep roof with dormers, a central pediment and Venetian windows in the salient end-pavilions. There is a watercolour drawing of it by H. G. Leask in the National Library of Ireland.

22   See Sir John Summerson in *Journal of the Royal Society of Arts* July 1959, p. 586 n26.

23   Photograph in the Welch Collection, Ulster Museum, Belfast. I saw the building both inside and out about 1940 ago, but it has since been destroyed.

24   In conversation. See G. A. Hayes McCoy, *Ulster and Other Irish Maps* Dublin 1964, e.g. Plate II and p. 3. Sometimes only the roofs are shown rounded while the walls are squared (as in some surviving examples) but in some cases the walls too are drawn as rounded and the houses look oval. A further complication is that many had post-and-wattle walls. Mr Danaher's opinion is certainly supported as regards early stone structures by the remains at Skellig Michael (see Leask, *Irish Churches* Vol 1, p. 14., and Liam de Paor in *Journal of the Royal Society of Antiquaries of Ireland* 1955, pp. 174-87) .

25   See the ravishingly beautiful photograph in Guinness and Ryan, *Irish Houses and Castles* p. 65.

26   See also E. M. Jope on the early use of brick in the North in *Ulster Journal of Archaeology* XXI, 1958, pp. 114-16 .

27   Howard Colvin and Maurice Craig (eds), *Architectural Drawings in the Library of Elton Hall, by Sir John Vanbrugh and Sir Edward Lovett Pearce* Oxford, for the Roxburghe Club 1964, No 146.

28   Measured drawing in *Georgian Society Records* Vol. V, Dublin 1913, plate CXXVI. I saw the house, still substantially existent, about twenty-five years ago.

29   A fine illustration is given in de Breffny and ffolliott, *op cit* 91.

30   K. Danaher, *Ireland's Vernacular Architecture,* pp 62, 63.

31   The derelict half-burnt roof of Clonfert Palace, Co. Galway may be a candidate.

32   Wilkinson. *Practical Geology and Ancient Architecture of Ireland* 1845, pp. 28–33 and 286.

33   Cloonbigny, Dundonnell and Tully are all about five miles from Ballinasloe; Gort is near Lecarrow and Athleague, its twin, is ten miles to the west; Lowberry is in the extreme west of the county near Cloonfad. A little to the west of Lecarrow, Kellybrook is inhabited though altered, and four miles west of Roscommon, Castle Coote, also inhabited, is in origin a 'star-fort' type stronghouse, remodelled in the 18th century. There are three or four more in a fragmentary state as well, in the same county.

34   Leask in *Studies in Building History* pp. 244-46; Craig in *Ulster Journal of Archaeology* 33, 1970, pp. 101-10 and plates XIII, XIV, and in *Journal of the Kildare Archaeological Society* XV, 1971, pp. 50-58 and plates VIII AND XI (same article reprinted)

35   Diaries in Drawings Collection of the RIBA: quoted by the Knight of Glin in *The Country Seat* p. 131.

36   For example at Drumcree, Co. Westmeath.

37   Castlemorres is illustrated in *Georgian Society Records* Vol. V 1913, plates CV-CVII.

38   Colvin and Craig *Vanbrugh-Pearce Drawings,* plates LVI and LXIV.

39   *Country Life* 21 and 28 May 1964, and Guinness and Ryan, *Irish Houses and Castles* pp. 39-47.

40   Illustrated in *Irish Georgian Society Bulletin* April-September 1967, plate 25.

41   If indeed both in *Apollo* October 1966, pp. 314-21.

42   The Knight of Glin in *Irish Georgian Society Bulletin* V, 1962, 11 sqq, an article otherwise sobered and superseded by the same writer's *Apollo* article cited in the preceding note.

43   For Davis Ducart's *oeuvre,* see the Knight of Glin in *Country Life* 26 September and 5 October 1967. Most of Ducart's houses are large, but Coole Abbey, Co. Cork, attributed to him, is quite small.

44   The Waringstown wings are probably additions, but early additions. There is no doubt about those at Jigginstown, Buncrana and Lismore.

45   See notes 41 and 42 above, for the articles by the Knight of Glin from which I cull the quotation.

46   *Monumental Classic Architecture in Great Britain and Ireland* London 1914, p. 28.

47   The drawings are in the National Library of Ireland, Dublin.

48   Ulster Architectural Heritage Society *North Derry* 1975, p. 39.

49   *Georgian Society Records* Vol. III 1911, Plate LXXXII.

50   See the photograph of Ballyknockan in Craig and Glin, *Ireland Observed,* p. 14.

51   Colvin and Craig *Vanbrugh-Pearce Drawings* plates XII, XIII, XIV, XXVI etc.

52   E. McParland, *Thomas Ivory Architect* Ballycotton 1973, p. 7.

53   Taylor and Skinner's *Maps of the Roads of Ireland* Dublin 1778, reprinted 1783. A most useful source for the ownership of houses, with a very long subscription list consisting no doubt principally of house-owners .

54   Donald Akenson, *The Church of Ireland ... 1800-1885* New Haven and London 1971, citing D. A. Beaufort, *Memoir of a Map of Ireland* Dublin and London 1792 (a much more comprehensive book than its modest title suggests).

55   Of these 354, no less than 202 were in the province of Armagh which, at the time, corresponded roughly to the political province of Ulster (nine counties)

56   See Sir John Betjeman in *The Pavilion* 1947 (to be treated with caution) and National Gallery of Ireland, Architectural Drawings Exhibition Catalogue 1975 no 54.

57   Illustrated in Craig and Glin, *Irish Architectural Drawings* 1965, No. 115.

58   Information of Rolf Loeber, and see his article in *Irish Georgian Society Bulletin* 1973, p. 37, and *Co. Down Archaeological Survey* Belfast 1966, p. 125, n173.

59   *Calendar of Ancient Records* of Dublin V, p. 306.

60   de Breffny and ffolliott, *Houses of Ireland* p. 90.

61   F. Elrington Ball, *The Correspondence of Jonathan Swift,* Vol. V, 1913, p. 295.

62   de Breffny and ffolliott, *Houses of Ireland* p. 98.

63   Information of the owner.

64   Drawings dated 1776 in the British Museum: see E. McParland, *Thomas Ivory Architect* Ballycotton 1973, pp. 7, 11.

65   Overlapping wings were used by Vanbrugh at his own house in Whitehall: *Vanbrugh-Pearce Drawings* plate XXVII. They occur also at St Paul's Waldenbury, illustrated by Reginald Tumor in *The Smaller English House* London 1952, plate 102, p. 93.

66   The Knight of Glin in *The Country Seat* p. 186.

BIBLIOGRAPHY

Bence-Jones, Mark *Burke's Guide to Country Houses: Ireland*, London 1978

Colvin, Howard and Maurice Craig, *Architectural Drawings in the Library of Elton Hall, by Sir John Vanbrugh and Sir Edward Lovett Pearce* Oxford, for the Roxburghe Club, 1964

Colvin, Howard and John Harris, (editors) *The Country Seat, Studies … presented to Sir John Summerson* London: The Penguin Press 1970

County Down Archaeological Survey Belfast: HMSO 1966

Craig, Maurice 'Some Smaller Irish Houses' *Country Life* 8 July 1949, pp. 131-32

Danaher, Kevin (Caoimhin Ó Danachair) *Ireland's Vernacular Architecture* Cork: Mercier Press 1975

de Breffny, Brian and Rosemary ffolliott, *Houses of Ireland* London: Thames and Hudson 1975

Glin, The Knight of (Desmond FitzGerald) 'Nathaniel Clements and Some Eighteenth-century Irish Houses' *Apollo* October 1966

Grove White, James *Historical and Topographical Notes* on [numerous localities in the baronies of north County Cork] 4 volumes, Cork 1905–25. A rich storehouse of photographs of houses in the richly endowed county of Cork: many of houses now destroyed

Evans, E. Estyn *Irish Heritage* Dundalk: The Dundalgan Press 1942

Humphreys, Thomas *The Irish Builder's Guide* Dublin 1813

Irish Ancestor, The (periodical) Dublin 1969 onwards

Irish Georgian Society Bulletin Dublin 1958 onwards

Jope, E. M. (editor) *Studies in Building History in Memory of B. H. St J. O'Neil* London: Odhams 1961 (contains two important articles, by H. G. Leask and D. M. Waterman)

Leask, H. G. *Irish Castles* Dundalk: The Dundalgan Press 1941 (and see also the preceding entry)

MacLysaght, Edward *Irish Life in the Seventeenth Century* Second, revised and enlarged edition: Cork University Press 1950

McParland, Edward 'Sir Richard Morrison's Country Houses' *Country Life* 24 and 31 May 1973

Morrison (Sir) Richard *Useful and Ornamental Designs in Architecture …*

Peculiarly Adapted for Execution Dublin:Robert Crosthwaite 1793

Payne, The Reverend John *Twelve Designs for Country Houses* Dublin 1757 (for the MS version, see pp. 39-49)

Stitt, William *The Practical Architect's Ready Assistant* Dublin, printed for the author, 1819

Taylor, George and Andrew Skinner, *Maps of the Roads of Ireland* Dublin 1778, reprinted 1783

Ulster Architectural Heritage Society: lists of buildings published from 1968 onwards

Waterman, D. M.: see above under Jope, E. M. (editor)

Wilkinson, George *Practical Geology and Ancient Architecture of Ireland* London and Dublin 1845. A very important but little-known book

INDEX

Figures in Italic refer to pages in which illustrations occur